EFFECTIVE READ-ALOUDS FOR EARLY LITERACY

Effective Read-Alouds for Early Literacy

A Teacher's Guide for PreK–1

Katherine A. Beauchat
Katrin L. Blamey
Zoi A. Philippakos

Foreword by Sharon Walpole

THE GUILFORD PRESS
New York   London

© 2012 The Guilford Press
A Division of Guilford Publications, Inc.
72 Spring Street, New York, NY 10012
www.guilford.com

Printed in the United States of America

This book is printed on acid-free paper.

Last digit is print number: 9   8   7   6   5   4   3   2   1

Library of Congress Cataloging-in-Publication Data

Effective read-alouds for early literacy : a teacher's guide for preK–1 / Katherine A. Beauchat . . . [et al.].
    p. cm.
  Includes bibliographical references and index.
  ISBN 978-1-4625-0396-4 (pbk.)
  1. Oral reading.   2. Language arts (Early childhood)   I. Beauchat, Katherine A.   II. Title.
  LB1573.5.E34 2012
  372.45′2—dc23
                                                                        2011049906

Par / teach
J
372.45
Bea
Main

To our families;
teachers of young children
for the important work that they do;
and our greatest teacher, Sharon Walpole

About the Authors

Katherine A. Beauchat, EdD, is Assistant Professor at York College of Pennsylvania, where she teaches undergraduate and graduate classes in literacy education. Her research interests include professional development for preschool educators in the area of literacy and language instruction and effective techniques and strategies to bolster at-risk preschool children's oral language and vocabulary development. Dr. Beauchat's recent publications include the coauthored article "Word Walk: A Vocabulary Strategy for Young Children" (*The Reading Teacher,* 2011); the book review "Preparing Teachers for the Early Childhood Classroom: Proven Models and Key Principles" (*NHSA Dialog,* 2011); the coauthored book *The Building Blocks of Preschool Success* (Guilford, 2010); the coauthored article "Building Preschool Children's Language and Literacy One Storybook at a Time" (*The Reading Teacher,* 2009); and the coauthored brief "Facilitating Teacher Study Groups" (*Literacy Coaching Clearinghouse,* 2008).

Katrin L. Blamey, PhD, is Assistant Professor of Education at DeSales University, Center Valley, Pennsylvania, where she teaches courses on early childhood literacy and elementary reading methods. Her research interests include finding effective, practical ways to implement professional development in the preschool setting and developing instructional techniques for building the language and literacy skills of preschool-age English language learners. Dr. Blamey's recent publications include the coauthored article "Word Walk: A Vocabulary Strategy for Young Children" (*The Reading Teacher,* 2011); the book review "Preparing Teachers for the Early Childhood Classroom: Proven Models and Key Principles" (*NHSA Dialog,* 2011); the coauthored book *The Building Blocks of Preschool Success* (Guilford, 2010); and the coauthored articles "Building Preschool Children's Language and Literacy One Storybook at a Time" (*The Reading Teacher,* 2009) and "Elementary Literacy Coaches: The Reality of Dual Roles" (*The Reading Teacher,* 2008).

Zoi A. Philippakos, MEd, is a doctoral student in literacy education at the University of Delaware. She has her master's degree in reading, has worked as an elementary school teacher and literacy coach, and provides professional development to teachers about effective reading and writing strategies. Her interests include reading and writing instruction for students in the elementary grades. Ms. Philippakos's recent publications include the coauthored book *Differentiated Reading Instruction in Grades 4 and 5: Strategies and Resources* (Guilford, 2011) and the coauthored article "Instruction in a Strategy for Compare–Contrast Writing" (*Exceptional Children*, 2010).

Foreword

As I think about the needs of our youngest readers and writers, I am always drawn to the needs of their teachers who choose to make preschool or the early primary classrooms home. This book is about your real needs as teachers, from the establishment of a special place and time for reading aloud to the nuts and bolts of turning the natural reading act into an intentional instructional opportunity.

In my own work with teachers, I have been surprised to hear them say, "I wish I still had time for read-alouds," or "To cover my content goals, I can't afford to waste time reading aloud." Their frustration stems from a failure of those of us who support teachers (perhaps myself included) to position the read-aloud as an essential context for language and literacy. Teachers who understand and are passionate about how and why they should read aloud will likely say that they could not meet an objective without it. The authors of this book fuel a passion for read-alouds, but they do so gently. It is my hope that this inspiration will keep that passion alive in spite of the other competing forces that tug at teachers' attention.

The book makes a strong case for the interdependence of receptive and expressive language. Thinking that relationship through is important to crafting a rationale for read-alouds. Discovering discrepancies in the oral language production of children who live in privileged literacy environments and those who do not is simple. You can hear the difference. But understanding that the source of the difference is the type, quality, and amount of language that surrounds the children is essential. Read-alouds alone will not address the lingering effects of poverty. What they will do, though, is provide all children with the opportunity to build on their existing language skills. The better the language children hear, the better the language they will understand, and, eventually, the better the language they will be able to produce. Better language exists in the books adults can read to children and in the talk that surrounds purposeful readings.

If you are still not convinced, wait until you read Chapter 8, on comprehension. As you read it, you can engage in an easy thought experiment. Consider the read-aloud, with both the words of the text *and* the talk provided by the teacher and children, as if it were the individual thinking that takes place in the mind of a skilled third-grade reader. It is really no different. A steady diet of interactive read-alouds during the first years of schooling provides a clear window into the thinking that accompanies skilled silent reading later. The more often a child looks through that window, the more likely he or she will be able to understand that reading is thinking.

Better performance in higher-order skills, especially for those children whose families live in poverty, is still elusive. Neither Early Reading First, a federally funded preschool initiative, nor Reading First, an initiative for kindergarten through third grade, have realized significant gains in children's oral language or comprehension. We cannot know for sure why that is so, but one possibility is the gulf between the recommendations of researchers and the daily work of teachers. These authors have built a bridge over that gulf. Their focus is evidence based, but they work as hard at implementation as they have at understanding research.

One thing that emerges from these pages is choice. These read-aloud plans are both consistent with research and easily adapted to the personal styles of teachers. Teachers, as much as students, need to feel comfortable trying new things, and these authors understand that concern. They also understand the complexity of the school day as they invite you to integrate what may be a very new practice into your existing routines. Finally, they understand that it is the achievement level of your children that should inform your instructional choices.

When we serve our youngest readers and writers, we may be tempted to focus too much attention on easily measured attainments. Alphabet knowledge, phonemic awareness, and decoding skills can be easily taught out of context, because children's response to instruction in these areas can be charted. Sometimes, the feedback that teachers receive—that their instructional efforts are yielding changes—can merit increased attention to those domains. Language and concept development skills, strategic skills, and the motivational benefits of high-quality, intentional read-alouds are not as easily measured. That does not mean, however, that their effects are not real and lasting. These authors are asking you to take a chance on children, to consider that if you invest time today, you are creating readers and writers tomorrow. This leap of faith is well justified in the research literature but sometimes difficult to appreciate in the day-to-day pressures of teaching.

I have found planning templates really helpful in organizing my own thinking about instruction, and these authors create templates for planning read-alouds that are both explicit and flexible. The templates in this book, though, are not add-ons. They form essential content that contextualizes ideas, one at a time. They present the authors' thinking in the context of a real-life instructional plan. They highlight choices and show that read-alouds can fuel the connectedness of ideas in a classroom community. I hope that you will spend time with the templates, really exploring the samples first and then creating your own.

If you spend time with this book, you will derive important research insights and practical supports for a reflective instructional cycle by reading the classroom vignettes. Reflection, as these authors are quick to point out, may not be natural for you. Reflection requires acceptance of mistakes and missed opportunities as a normal part of instruction. The vignettes of classroom teachers presented here are artful in their completeness. They guide you through all stages—from book selection to planning to implementation to reflection—such that you can really see and hear teachers reading aloud in voices that sound natural and sometimes flawed, like authentic interactions with children. For me, the detail provided in the vignettes makes these read-alouds hard to resist.

Perhaps as a measure of these authors' understanding of and respect for teachers, they invite you to rediscover the titles in your classroom library for new purposes; to consider the needs of your children before you decide how to harness the power of children's literature; to start small, with only one target skill, and then to try targeting more than one; to reflect on both the strengths and weaknesses of a given lesson; and, finally, to change the skills you emphasize as your children's skills grow.

With a good book in your hand, consider these invitations: Let's talk! Wonderful words make a difference! Let's understand how print works! Let's learn the alphabet! Let's focus on sounds! And let's get to the heart of it all: comprehension. You will find that this book, like a good read-aloud, is one that you will revisit. Your children need you to.

SHARON WALPOLE, PhD
University of Delaware

Preface

In Mo Willems's *We Are in a Book!* (2010), the latest addition to his Elephant and Piggie series for beginning readers, the main characters Elephant and Piggie discover that they are, as the title suggests, *in* a book. Elephant declares that being in a book is "so cool!" while jocular Piggie decides to have some fun with the reader by making the reader say a funny word—*banana* . Elephant is amazed that Piggie can make a reader do something and wonders how Piggie can do it, to which Piggie replies, "I can. If the reader reads out loud."

"If the reader reads out loud." For the authors of this book, Mo Willems's clever conceit is not only amusing but also powerful. As literacy educators and researchers, we know how important reading out loud to children can be for developing crucial literacy skills such as phonological awareness, concepts of print, alphabet knowledge, oral language, vocabulary, and comprehension. Equally compelling is our knowledge as aunts, mothers, and grandmothers of young children. We have seen our own children experience the joy of listening to great literature being read aloud. We have firsthand knowledge of what it looks like when a baby first begins to notice the pictures in an Eric Carle book, to use his or her tiny finger to point to a word on the page of a board book, to giggle in delight at the rhythm of a good rhyming book, and to crawl into our laps at the end of the day to hear a favorite bedtime story. It is safe to say that reading out loud to children is our passion.

The genesis of this book came after several years of working with teachers reading out loud to children of all different ages and grade levels. Collectively we have worked with preschool, K–6 elementary, and 7–9 middle school teachers in planning and implementing literacy instruction. A teaching method constant across this wide span of grade levels is the classic classroom read-aloud. While the literacy skills, concepts, or strategies emphasized change, depending on the students and the grade level, the basic elements of the read-aloud remain consistent. The read-aloud is a time in the hectic classroom schedule when the school day seems to slow down just a bit and the tone of the classroom changes as students settle down on a reading rug or at their desks to listen as the teacher reads a storybook, nonfiction text, anthology selection, or any relevant piece of text out loud. The beauty of the read-aloud is its versatility.

You can imagine a read-aloud in any classroom. A preschool teacher leading a unit on space can read aloud a nonfiction text on the moon to young children, pausing to discuss wonderful space-related vocabulary. A kindergarten teacher developing students' phonological awareness can read aloud a rhyming text for students to identify rhyme. A second-grade teacher building students' repertoire of comprehension strategies can read aloud a sequential text for students to retell. A fourth-grade teacher can read aloud a primary document for students to learn about the Revolutionary War. The list of possibilities is endless; for every learning objective that exists, there also exists a text that can be read aloud and discussed to meet the objective.

One reason we began writing this book was to help you realize the incredible potential of the read-aloud as an instructional classroom practice in the prekindergarten through grade 1 classroom. You really would be hard-pressed to think of a topic or skill for which a corresponding book to read aloud does not exist to supplement your instruction. At the same time, reading aloud high-quality literature to children is an absolutely joyful experience. Children of all ages enjoy listening to good books. Not only can classroom read-alouds be instructionally purposeful and powerful, but they can also be pleasurable for both you and your students. Subsequent chapters of this book discuss methods for infusing literacy instruction into the read-aloud experience; however, at no time while reading about and implementing these practices do we want you to ever forget the joy that reading aloud should bring to all participants. Reading aloud can meet instructional objectives, develop children's literacy skills, and be joyful.

A second reason we undertook writing this book was to help you in planning instruction, as you consider the instructional goals of your school and the guidelines described in your state standards or the newly adopted national Common Core State Standards (CCSS) (National Governors Association Center for Best Practices and Council of Chief State School Officers, 2010). These standards set specific expectations for students from prekindergarten to grade 1 in the areas of phonological awareness, print awareness, phonics, vocabulary, and comprehension. This book addresses those expectations and utilizes research findings, giving you the tools to thoughtfully plan and reflect on the specific skills that are necessary for the development of these areas of literacy. Chapter 1 discusses each of the areas of literacy and how they fit broadly within the read-aloud context. As you read through the remaining chapters, you will discover that each is devoted to a single area, discussing how you can plan, implement, and reflect on a read-aloud that addresses a key literacy skill or skills. We discuss how to prepare your classroom and your schedule for read-alouds (Chapter 2), read-aloud practices for developing oral language (Chapter 3), vocabulary (Chapter 4), book and print conventions (Chapter 5), alphabet awareness (Chapter 6), phonological awareness (Chapter 7), and comprehension (Chapter 8).

Working with teachers across grade levels, we know how important and scarce planning time can be. Therefore, a third goal of this book is to provide you with practical, easy-to-use planning templates for supporting your work with literacy-infused read-alouds. The Appendix includes planning templates that can be reproduced and used again and again as you think about which literacy skills to target and emphasize during your classroom read-alouds. As a reminder, the planning templates provide a list of research-based best practices for developing each skill. To support your use of the planning template, each chapter includes a discussion of best practices and why they work and an illustrative case study of a teacher using the practices during an example read-aloud. As you listen to the teachers in our case studies reading aloud, imagine how you could also develop literacy skills by reading other wonderful books you and your students enjoy. As added support, we also provide a list of fiction and nonfiction books that can develop or address the targeted skill.

We know that planning must include an element of reflection to be effective. Therefore, each chapter embeds the planning template within a cycle of planning, implementing, and then reflecting on your classroom read-aloud. The reflection we propose makes use of your initial plan and assessment information about your students. As you read aloud with your students, collecting important information about their participation and involvement will help you reflect so as to determine their levels of understanding and to plan future instruction. Assessment information during a read-aloud could be formal but can also include observational data. For example, during your instruction you can keep notes on students' performance in relation to your goals and learning objectives. Soon after the end of your lesson, during a lunch or planning break, you may respond critically and redefine your goals or restructure the form of your lesson delivery to better meet the needs of your students. You may find that students have mastered the concept or skill you intended and that your next read-aloud needs to be more challenging, or you may find that some students continue to struggle with a skill and that revisiting the skill in your next read-aloud will be beneficial. We know that when time is precious, planning and reflecting may seem like a lot of work. Therefore, we have embedded reflection right into the planning templates included in this book. We hope that the reflection column of the planning template will help remind you to think about how students responded to your instruction so that you can be in a powerful position to set data-driven goals for your very next read-aloud.

We have discussed how the chapters in this book consider a literacy skill in isolation and examine how a teacher can plan and reflect upon a read-aloud targeting a key area of literacy. We have also discussed the instructional possibility of the read-aloud format. Therefore, the goal of the book's concluding chapter is to acknowledge teachers' great ability to multitask. Chapter 9 considers how read-alouds and repeated readings of the same text can enable you to develop multiple literacy skills simultaneously. Savvy combinations of literacy skills targeted during a read-aloud that are appropriate to the text selected and to students' needs can meet the multiple learning objectives you have for your students at any given time. We made an organizational decision to discuss each literacy area separately first and then in combination to allow for a thorough discussion of each skill within the read-aloud context. As you read each chapter in sequence, keep in mind that the last chapter discusses combining skills into a single read-aloud. Or, you may decide to skip ahead and read Chapter 9 first to see how it all fits together before going back to learn about each skill in more depth.

We have set several goals for ourselves in the following pages. We hope to convince you of the incredible instructional potential and joy of reading aloud to children. We hope to help you make conscious decisions about how to target literacy skills in your instruction to meet the expectations of grade-level standards and address the guidelines set by the CCSS. We hope to provide you with practical, useful templates for planning, reflecting upon, and setting instructional goals for read-alouds in your classroom. Finally, we hope to spark your thinking about how to make wise decisions about combining literacy targets in the same or repeated read-alouds.

Returning to Mo Willems's endearing characters, as Piggie explains to an astonished, and perhaps heartbroken, Elephant, all books end. We hope that as you end your reading of this book you will begin your journey reading aloud to children. So, the next time you pick up a great piece of children's literature, think of the profound words of Elephant, "I just want to be read," and consider the endless possibilities that a literacy-infused read-aloud can bring to the children in your classroom. Happy reading aloud!

Contents

EFFECTIVE READ-ALOUDS FOR EARLY LITERACY

CHAPTER 1

Using Read-Alouds to Build Early Literacy and Language Success

Read-alouds set up children for literacy success. Research and practice show that reading aloud to young children is the best way to prepare children for learning to read and to keep them reading as they learn and grow. Reading aloud helps children develop the critical literacy and language skills that they will use in school and throughout their lives.

Why Read-Alouds Are the Perfect Context

Reading aloud is often children's first entrance into discovering the wonderful world of literacy. It creates a unique bonding experience between the reader and the listener only shared through the pages of a book. As parents, caregivers, and teachers read aloud they nurture children's love of both the written and spoken word. Read-alouds stimulate children's imagination and curiosity as they follow the twists and turns of a plot or discover new facts and ideas. It also helps children develop the important oral language skills that will help them learn to read and write on their own. See Figure 1.1 for additional benefits of read-alouds. Ultimately, read-alouds develop children's lifelong appreciation for reading.

Read-alouds are also the common thread that ties all early childhood classrooms together. There's a good reason for this. Research is especially rich on the impact and effectiveness of reading aloud and the research is abundantly clear: young children who are read to on a consistent basis are provided the tools for future literacy and language success (e.g., Bus & van IJzendoorn, 1995; Wells, 1986). The International Reading Association and the National Association for the Education of Young Children (IRA/NAEYC) concur and state, "The single most important activity for

- Provide exposure to rich, authentic literature.
- Develop children's motivation and appreciation for reading.
- Provide authentic opportunities for parents and teachers to model what good readers do.
- Develop children's understandings of the forms and functions of print.
- Provide opportunities for language and vocabulary expansion.
- Develop children's imagination, curiosity, and comprehension of text.

FIGURE 1.1. Benefits of read-alouds.

building these understandings and skills essential for reading success appears to be reading aloud to children" (1998, p. 198).

Key Targets to Develop through Read-Alouds

The research literature argues that read-alouds can enhance essential emergent literacy and language skills. It also suggests that early childhood educators can maximize the potential of read-alouds when they realize the gains that can be made through targeted instruction of these skills during the read-aloud experience. These include read-alouds as a rich context for fostering children's oral language and vocabulary development, comprehension development, and print and alphabet awareness, as well as phonological awareness. See Figure 1.2 for the literacy and language target skills that can be developed in read-alouds. In the following sections we provide a brief overview on each of these key language and literacy skills and the rationale for enhancing them in the read-aloud experience.

Developing Oral Language and Vocabulary

Oral language and vocabulary lay the foundation for young children's literacy and language development. Language development is natural. Young children are

- Oral language development
- Vocabulary development
- Comprehension development
- Print awareness
- Alphabet awareness
- Phonological awareness

FIGURE 1.2. Skills developed through read-alouds.

naturally hardwired to learn the language they hear in their environment, and they tend to progress through predictable stages and milestones of language development fairly consistently across all populations. However, the quantity and quality of children's language and vocabulary is not natural. A landmark research study by Hart and Risley (1995) found that children are exposed to vastly different language and vocabulary experiences and that these experiences and exposures are highly connected to socioeconomic status. In effect, children from low-income homes remain well behind their more economically advantaged peers when they enter school and as they progress through school. By grade 1 the gap between less and more economically advantaged students is approximately 1,200 words; however, by grade 3 the gap increases to approximately 2,500 words. The good news is that if teachers make concerted and conscientious efforts to bolster children's language and vocabulary, this gap can be narrowed early.

A well-documented practice that holds much potential for accomplishing this goal is reading aloud. Research suggests that read-alouds that occur frequently and contain high levels of adult–child discussion surrounding the story and the vocabulary words targeted within the book can increase children's listening and speaking vocabulary (e.g., Aram, 2006; Elley, 1989; Justice, Meier, & Walpole, 2005; Robbins & Ehri, 1994).

Early childhood educators who are aware of the rich and meaningful potential to build language and vocabulary during the read-aloud experience engage in a number of activities that can support vocabulary growth. These educators can be observed asking open-ended questions, repeating, expanding, and recasting children's utterances, and taking on the role of listener so that the child becomes the storyteller (e.g., Whitehurst et al., 1994). They also seize the vocabulary potential within the read-alouds, conducting rich and meaningful discussions about words that they have chosen from the book so that children can add these words to their vocabulary stores (e.g., Beck & McKeown, 2007; Walsh & Blewitt, 2006; Wasik & Bond, 2001).

These collective practices are important for early childhood educators, particularly those who work with a language- and vocabulary-disadvantaged population. However, such practices do require thoughtful planning. Read-alouds should be carefully planned and structured with the goal to increase the amount of talk surrounding the events of the read-aloud and the words within the book so that children are provided consistent opportunities to grow their language and vocabulary.

Developing Print and Alphabetic Awareness

Another essential component of young children's literacy development lies in the area of print and alphabetic knowledge (e.g., Justice, Bowles, & Skibbe, 2006; Lovelace & Stewart, 2007; Morris, Bloodgood, & Perney, 2003). In order for children to move into literacy and reading development they must possess critical skills such as print- and book-reading knowledge (e.g., left-to-right directionality of print), concept of word (ability to match the written word with the spoken word), and alphabetic knowledge (knowing the features and names of the letters of the alphabet). The National Early Literacy Panel (NELP) found that in addition to phonological awareness, print knowledge was one of the strongest predictors of a child's early success in reading (2007). However, growth in print awareness is highly dependent upon exposure to and engagement with various print functions and forms (Neuman, 1999).

The role of early childhood educators is critical for the development of this component of literacy as well. Early childhood educators can optimize the potential of read-alouds and provide these multiple exposures to written language, specifically in the area of print and alphabet awareness. Early childhood educators who are aware of the potential to target print and alphabet awareness during the read-aloud experience can be observed modeling concepts such as left-to-right and top-to-bottom progression, tracking print, differentiating between a letter and a word, and drawing attention to specific letters of the alphabet (IRA/NAEYC, 1998; Pullen & Justice, 2003; Uhry, 2002). They also optimize the powerful potential of read-alouds and encourage children to become active, rather than passive, in the event. In this respect, children can often be observed coming up to the book, most often big books, to point out and display their print and alphabet awareness knowledge. These experiences not only develop children's sense of accomplishment and pride but they help to pave the road toward becoming a successful reader.

Developing Phonological Awareness

Read-alouds provide rich and playful opportunities for children to focus attention on the sound structure of language-phonological awareness. Phonological awareness refers to a child's ability to reflect on and manipulate the sounds in our language, including rhymes, syllables, initial sounds, onset–rimes, and, finally, individual phonemes in words (Adams, 1990; Vellutiono & Scanlon, 1987). This awareness requires children to switch attention from the meanings of words to the sounds of words. As children move through these elements of phonological awareness they realize that language is made up of words, words are made up of sounds, or phonemes, and these sounds are connected to letters and letter patterns. Phonological awareness lays this critical foundational for children to learn spelling–sound correspondences (Adams, 1990). Essentially, phonological awareness helps children to learn to read and spell.

Many children become aware of early forms of phonological awareness incidentally through daily experiences with nursery rhymes, rhyming poems and books, and word play (Lonigan, Burgess, Anthony, & Barker, 1998). However, because phonological awareness exerts such a strong impact on children's short- and long-term reading development, it's best not to leave exposures to this skill to chance (Yopp & Yopp, 2000). Research findings on phonological awareness suggest that children in the emergent literacy stage with the strongest phonological awareness are most likely to become the strongest and most successful readers. Conversely, children in this stage with the poorest phonological awareness are likely to become the poorest readers (Ball & Blachman, 1991; Juel, 1988; Stanovich, 1986). The heartening news is that if phonological deficits are targeted early in children's reading career, they are amenable to instruction (Adams, 1990; NAEYC/IRA, 1998; National Reading Panel [NRP], 2000).

Read-alouds are an ideal context in which to develop these critical phonological awareness skills. Early childhood educators who are aware of the potential to target phonological awareness during the read-aloud experience can be observed calling children's attention to rhymes, syllables, and beginning sounds and alliteration, as well as letter–sound correspondences in words. These consistent exposures to phonological awareness go a long way in developing children's awareness of the sound structure of language. Taken together, these findings indicate that targeted attention during the context of the read-aloud experience provides multiple opportunities for children to develop phonological awareness, a necessary precursor to unlocking the code in their first reading and spelling attempts (NRP, 2000; Yopp & Yopp, 2000).

Developing Comprehension

Comprehension is the reason for reading. Children's reading success and achievements will be measured according to whether they can derive meaning from print (Snow, 2002). The read-aloud experience presents the perfect place to foster children's comprehension development. It provides a time for meaningful adult–child and peer–peer exchanges and active participation surrounding the reading event. These discussions occur before, during, and after reading the book and work toward enhancing children's comprehension and sense of text structure (McGee & Schickedanz, 2007; Pressley & Hilden, 2002). Young children may not have the capability to read complex books independently but they can certainly listen to a book with a complex plot and engage in thoughtful discussion.

It's important to keep in mind that rich adult–child and peer–peer discussion doesn't happen by accident. Early childhood educators who optimize the potential for discussion that targets children's comprehension model analytical thinking and ask questions that reflect children's interest and have many potential responses, rather than just one correct answer. They carefully plan the read-aloud to include predictions, open-ended questions, questions that connect to children's lives and experiences, questions that make connections between characters and acts of different books, and require children to reflect on what was read to construct meaning before, during, and after the reading event (Pressley & Hilden, 2002). In effect, they model that reading is thinking. They also require children to be actively engaged in the read-aloud so that children learn that reading is thinking.

Another technique for developing children's comprehension is through repeated readings of the same book. It's certainly true that children love to have their favorite book read time and time again. This practice is assumed to build a sense of comfort and familiarity. This love of repetition also has its advantages in the context of storybook reading—it fosters comprehension. Children who have been exposed to repeated readings of one book gradually increase the sophistication of their responses after each subsequent reading (McGee & Schickedanz, 2007). They can be observed providing responses that are more interpretive and elaborative and making more judgments about the characters, events, and resolutions (e.g., Bus, 2001). Also, planned repeated readings engage children in rich discussions that increase their expressive and oral language (Trachtenburg & Ferruggia, 1989). Truly, carefully planned read-alouds are one of the best ways to develop young children's comprehension of text. Engaging in multiple or repeated readings of one book may be the most effective way to ensure children are provided with consistent opportunities to derive meaning from print.

Final Thoughts

Read-alouds are a highly valued adult–child literacy experience—shared both at home and in the classroom. It's often children's first experience with literacy and fosters positive attitudes and motivation toward wanting to be a reader. We also know that read-alouds hold the potential to build children's literacy and language skills. These skills, including oral language and vocabulary development, print and alphabet awareness, phonological awareness, and comprehension have asserted themselves as critical areas needed for children's literacy success. Ensuring that children are provided with targeted instruction of these skills in read-alouds require educators to plan and reflect. In the remaining chapters of this book, we provide you with the necessary knowledge and tools to assist you in making the most out of your very next read-aloud.

CHAPTER 2

Preparing for Read-Alouds in the Classroom

With a little preparation reading aloud with students can be truly rewarding. As discussed in the preceeding chapter, read-alouds offer the opportunity for infusing literacy instruction into a meaningful context. Preparing for the read-aloud experience includes consideration of your classroom space set aside specifically for reading and the time you build into your classroom schedule for reading. Thinking about the components of effective read-alouds in general will help ensure student engagement. In addition, an important part of preparation is working through the instructional cycle of planning, implementing, and then reflecting on the read-aloud in order to set goals for improvement. Considering these aspects of preparing for read-alouds ahead of time will help set the stage for effective literacy-infused read-alouds in your classroom.

Creating a Space for Read-Alouds

As educators we can learn a lot from bookstores. Booksellers know how to create an atmosphere just right for reading. Think about the last time you walked through a great bookstore. Bookshelves line the walls. Books with appealing covers are organized facing out for the casual passerby to spot an intriguing title or cover photo. Colorful posters cover the walls advertising the newest "must reads." Underfoot plush carpeting makes it easy to walk. Big comfortable chairs create cozy little nooks for you to plop down with a stack of books you are considering reading. The lighting is soft, not too bright or jarring. There is a scent of paper and coffee and perhaps a hint of chocolate chip cookies in the air. And not only are there books but also stationery and pens and soft stuffed animals for sale.

While you probably cannot bake chocolate chip cookies every day in your classroom, you can set the stage for reading by taking some lessons from booksellers. Figure 2.1 provides some guiding questions for creating your perfect read-aloud space in the classroom. First, preview the physical layout of your classroom and look for a space that has good lighting. A spot near a window may make a bright and cheery reading corner. A location accessible to an electrical outlet where you can place a nice reading lamp may be ideal. Above all make sure there is enough light to see what you are reading.

A second important physical consideration is size. Of course you need a spot large enough to fit all of the children in your classroom for whole-group read-alouds. However, remember what booksellers know, that cozy spots are also conducive for reading. Find a balance in size of your reading area between big enough to comfortably fit all your students and limited enough to create a cozy feel. We have found that if an area is too big it easily becomes a place for a lot of movement; children may be tempted to try out their latest gymnastic moves rather than find a great book to listen to or read independently.

While you may have students read independently in a separate library corner or at their desks, the large-group reading area can set the mood for reading with a few additional materials. If you have a bookshelf to spare from your library corner, adding a bookshelf to the large-group reading area may help to create a boundary between one area in the classroom and the reading area and is also a great way to put the focus on reading. Especially if you have big books for reading to the whole group and curriculum materials from your reading program, it is important to have adequate storage. You may choose to leave some books out for children to explore on their own after large-group time. You may also decide to keep some materials out of reach for safekeeping. Whatever your decision, it is important to have materials easily accessible when you need them for your own reading instruction. We have seen teachers successfully use bookshelves, baskets, plastic tubs, cabinets, and easels in their book areas to create easy-to-reach storage.

For your space in the reading area, create an inventory of the materials you will need on a daily basis. You will probably need reading materials like books and

- What is the lighting like in the area? Is there adequate lighting for reading?
- How large is the space? Can all of my students comfortably fit?
- How will reading materials be stored and accessed in the space?
- Where will you sit comfortably to read to the group?
- Where will students sit? How will they know where to sit?
- What decorations can you add to create an inviting space for literacy instruction?
- Are there any other props or special touches you can add to create your perfect read-aloud space for you and your students?

FIGURE 2.1. Thinking about read-aloud spaces.

reading pointers. You may use writing materials like chart paper and markers. You will certainly need a spot on the floor or a nice chair to sit in. Since you will be using the area every day, consider investing in a really comfortable chair so that you can look forward to reading there. We have seen kindergarten and first-grade classrooms with rocking chairs, armchairs, and teacher-sized folding chairs that work well for the reading area. One consideration when choosing teacher seating is to make sure you are not so far away from the students that they can no longer see the book. For example, sitting on a tall stool above students seated on the floor may not be ideal for allowing good viewing opportunities.

Thinking about the plush carpeting in those great bookstores we love to frequent, consider adding a small carpet to your reading area. Have you ever considered that children may become fidgety while listening to you read because they are uncomfortable on the floor? A nice thick carpet can help make students more comfortable while sitting to listen to your reading. It can also create the cozy feel we are trying to create as our reading atmosphere. Similarly, you may want to throw in some carpet squares, alphabet tiles, or colorful pillows to help create distinct reading spots for students to sit. You can really cut down on the amount of time it takes to get organized for reading if students know exactly where to sit. With some groups of children it can be helpful to have a bit of space between seats to minimize the amount of personal interaction and, therefore, distraction.

Decorating the walls around the reading area can help to promote the space as one dedicated to literacy. Of course there are fantastic wall posters available at teacher stores and online through library associations. Another option is to post illustrations or book covers from students' favorite authors. We also recommend using student work to decorate the reading area over the course of the year. Students love seeing their own work around the room; it sends them the message that their writing is important and valued. From an educational perspective, posting student work helps to cement the concept of print idea that written text conveys meaning.

Finally, as an added touch think about what elements or props you can add to make the reading area even more cozy and inviting. Because you and your students will be using the area every day, it is worth it to add those extra little touches to make the space special. Think about what bookstores include or the elements you have included in the reading nook of your own house. These may be green plants, flowers, soft stuffed animals from favorite books, paper and writing utensils, or pillows. Remember that the reading area is a central spot in your classroom for instruction and gathering together as a large group, the amount of time and care you spend planning it will be returned threefold when you and your students genuinely enjoy being there to read and discuss books together.

Creating Time for Read-Alouds

Once you have created your ideal reading area, the next thing to consider before students even begin the year in your classroom is creating your reading routine.

Setting an appropriate reading routine and getting students on that routine as early as possible will go a long way for helping establish healthy classroom behavior and management.

A good read-aloud for PreK and primary students varies in length, but a good rule of thumb is between 15 and 25 minutes long. At the beginning of the year when students are adapting to their new classroom and the new reading tasks asked of them, it may be a good idea to keep the read-aloud shorter. Once students are comfortable with the read-aloud format, you may decide that students will be able to handle a longer reading time. Keep in mind too that every group of students is different, and you need to think about the unique characteristics of your class when making decisions about timing. In addition, certain events may occur during the school day that may throw off the flow of your day, therefore changing your reading schedule. School assemblies, fire drills, book carnivals, or sporting events may cause you to make adjustments in the duration of your read-aloud. Remaining flexible when necessary will help you maintain your sanity; maintaining an organized structure whenever possible will help you establish order and expectations for reading.

Another important consideration for establishing a time for reading is the time of day that is best suited for reading instruction. This decision may depend on your overall school schedule and when reading specialists or support persons are available to you. The decision may also be based on knowledge of your students. Will they listen and attend to reading in a large group better first thing in the morning or after lunch? Will they be attentive after centers or outdoor play? You may want to establish multiple times to read aloud during the school day schedule. The more opportunities students have to listen to read-alouds in the classroom the better. If your schedule affords the opportunity for multiple read-alouds, consider spacing the read-alouds apart so that students have adequate time to move about in between periods when they are expected to sit still for reading.

We recommend a few guiding questions to think about when establishing a reading routine. Figure 2.2 summarizes these questions. First, how will students know when to go to the reading area? Consider creating a master classroom schedule with the read-aloud occurring at close to the same time every day so students can become accustomed to listening and interacting to a read-aloud at that time of the day. Consider how you will transition students from their desks or other parts

- How will students know when to go to the reading area?
- Where will students sit? Will there be a seating arrangement?
- How will students sit during the reading?
- What will students be expected to do during the read-aloud?
- How will students know when to change their behavior during the read-aloud?
- How will the read-aloud end? How will students exit the reading area?

FIGURE 2.2. Thinking about read-aloud routines.

of the classroom to the reading area in an organized way. Will you dismiss students rows at a time to the reading area? Will you ask students to go by responding to a question, such as the letter in their name, the color they are wearing, or whether they are a boy or a girl?

Next, think about the seating arrangement. You want to anticipate whether there are students who should not sit together because they are prone to distracting one another. You also will want to anticipate whether there are students who need to sit up front in order to see or to be close to you for behavior management. If there is a seating arrangement, how will it be indicated to the students? Will you put student names on the floor of the reading area? Will you tell students where their spot is and ask them to sit there consistently? Will you allow students to seat themselves? Also consider how students should sit during the reading. Many teachers insist students sit with their legs crossed in front of them so to leave space for other students to sit and for students to walk by to complete reading or writing tasks.

The best read-aloud routine begins with clear expectations. The expectations you have for creating a read-aloud experience are your own and will naturally vary according to teacher. Some teachers ask students to raise their hands before responding to questions, while other teachers allow students to call out their answers. Some teachers are fine with student movement during the reading; other teachers prefer students to be more still. Determine what your own limits are, and then, most important, communicate these expectations for behavior to your students. Taking time to establish the expectations at the beginning of the school year will really set the tone for every subsequent read-aloud throughout the year. It is worth taking the time to make sure every student understands what good reading behavior looks like. You may want to establish reading behavior through discussion, by writing a list of expectations with students to post in the reading area, or by acting out good and poor reading behavior with student participants. Involving students in the decision-making process is one strategy teachers use to help make students feel responsible for their own behavior. If students have helped to create the expectations, then they may be even more likely to view them as important.

Just as you have management routines for the rest of the school day, it is important to have mechanisms for encouraging students to redirect their behavior during reading. You can gently call a student's name, tap a student on the shoulder, make direct eye contact, or praise good behavior when you see it during the reading in order to alert students to how they should behave while listening to read-alouds. Whatever habit you choose for maintaining your expectations, remember that consistency is important when working with students of all ages. If you are clear with your expectations for reading behavior and consistently expect the same behavior from students, they will be more likely to act accordingly.

Finally, think about how to end your reading time. Rather than simply ending by finishing reading a book, consider establishing a daily ending. You may want to summarize what you did during the reading time, or you may want to end by reading a daily poem or writing a morning message. You may ask students to respond to a question about the book or the reading activities before ending the reading. Also think about how students will exit the reading area. Will you dismiss all the students at the same time? Will you ask students to go a row at a time? Think about ending the reading with clear directions for what activities students will go to next in order to minimize classroom upheaval.

Components of Effective Read-Alouds

Once you have created a space for large-group reading in your classroom and planned a time for reading in your schedule, the next step is thinking about how to make read-alouds engaging for young students. A good read-aloud begins with a good book. There are so many high-quality children's fiction and nonfiction books available that it can be difficult and time consuming to sort through the choices. In the chapters that follow we describe characteristics of books that are useful for targeting the specific literacy elements outlined in the previous chapter. In addition, we share with you some of the children's book titles and authors we have enjoyed reading with young children. Certainly, nothing can compare to finding books that you know your specific group of students will enjoy. Use your knowledge of the special interests and experiences of your students to help you identify books that they will enjoy hearing and discussing.

We like to think of the read-aloud experience in terms of what happens before, during, and after reading (see Figure 2.3). As discussed in the section above, it is

Before Reading
• Begin with a good book selection—what book will match both your literacy instruction and your students' interests well?
• Restate your expectations for good read-aloud behavior.
• Capture students' attention through discussion or providing a concrete prop of an idea related to the text.
During Reading
• Be enthusiastic.
• Be expressive.
• Be dramatic.
• Weave in meaningful literacy instruction.
• Involve the audience through participation.
After Reading
• Summarize the central idea of the text.
• Summarize the literacy skill or skills you practiced.
• Ask students what they thought about the text and why.

FIGURE 2.3. The before, during, and after reading cycle.

always a good idea to begin a read-aloud by clearly restating expectations for reading behavior. This can be done very quickly but can go a long way toward setting a positive tone for the entire read-aloud. Before reading is also a perfect opportunity to capture students' attention by getting them interested in the book you will be reading. This may mean asking students a question to see whether they have ever experienced anything like what happens in the book. It may mean describing something new to students to build their background knowledge prior to reading. For young students it can be especially helpful to share a prop or picture or action with students before reading.

A powerful reader captivates his or her audience during reading. Borrowing a few techniques from drama, you can engage your students by performing the read-aloud. First, be enthusiastic. Even the youngest child will recognize when you are excited to be reading. When you are unenthusiastic, your attitude will rub off on your students. Next, fill your voice with expression. If you are reading a book with dialogue, give characters different voices to help distinguish the speaking roles for students who are listening. Make sure you raise your voice at the end of a question and add excitement to sentences ending with exclamation points. Also, think about adding small props as visuals or making sound effects when appropriate. For example, if there is a knock at the door, use your fist to knock so that students can actually hear the sounds from the story. Finally, have a plan for audience participation. Depending on the literacy element you are targeting during your read-aloud, your plan for audience participation will differ. In the chapters that follow we outline the best practices identified by research as methods for engaging students in the practice of each of the major literacy elements during read-alouds.

After reading it is always a good idea to review the literacy element you introduced and practiced with students. Give a brief summary of not only what you read but also what you practiced. For example, you may conclude with, "Today we read a great book about a bear that went on an exciting adventure. We also practiced thinking about rhyming words while we read. Remember, rhyming words are words that have the same ending sounds." After reading is also a good time for gauging whether or not students enjoyed the book, which will help you in turn decide on books for future read-alouds. A simple question about whether or not students enjoyed the book and why can help spark conversation around literature from even the youngest children and is a great way to develop discerning readers.

In the chapters that follow we describe and provide examples of implementing best practices in literacy instruction during the context of read-alouds. As you read our examples and begin to construct your own lesson plans, keep in mind the general components of effective read-alouds described here for before, during, and after reading. It can be tempting to focus on a specific literacy element to such an extent that the big picture of the overall read-aloud is lost. This may mean extensive practice with one skill can detract from the overall flow and enjoyment of the reading experience. We urge you to retain the enjoyment of the experience for yourself and your students as you also weave in meaningful literacy instruction into your read-alouds.

Introducing the Planning, Implementing, and Reflecting Cycle

Having created the space and the classroom time for reading aloud with students and then thought about the big-picture elements that make read-alouds effective, the next step is to actually enter the cycle of planning, implementing, and reflecting upon your instruction. We strongly believe that thinking about instruction in terms of the planning you do before teaching, the steps that you take while teaching, and the reflective thinking you do after teaching is a worthwhile exercise in which all teachers—from beginners to experts—participate to strengthen their craft. Let's briefly consider each element of the cycle.

Weaving research-based practices into your read-aloud takes planning. To implement the activities described in the remainder of this book, you simply cannot pick a children's book up off a shelf and expect to present instruction of the elements effectively without planning. A good read-aloud requires thinking ahead of time about the fit between the activities you wish to implement and the text you will be reading. In addition, you will want to think about the level and stage of your students in order to create a comfortable match with the type of activity you choose to engage them in while learning the literacy element. For example, if you are working with young prekindergartners near the beginning of the year, you will probably want to model a print convention for them rather than ask them to label a print convention on their own. Creating your lesson plan also requires thinking about exactly when during the read-aloud—before, during, or after—is appropriate for engaging students in the instructional activity. You will want to read and reread the book to determine on which page you will pause to engage students in a specific learning activity.

To help facilitate your planning of read-alouds, we have included in Chapters 3–8 a planning template created specifically for implementing the best practices associated with each literacy element. For example, Chapter 3, on oral language includes a planning template created to help you design read-alouds targeting students' oral language development. In each chapter we spend time describing the best practices included in the planning template so that you can begin to feel comfortable planning your own instruction. A blank planning template for each literacy element is provided for your own use in the book's Appendix.

Following from a plan is actual implementation of the read-aloud with students. Implementation involves actually using the plan you took the time to create for the read-aloud ahead of time to the best that the classroom circumstances allow. Of course we have all been in the situation where our best thought-out lesson plan must be altered because of an unannounced school assembly or an unanticipated reaction from the students. Those unforeseen events are an inevitable reality of teaching, which is why we acknowledge that implementing a lesson plan to the exact letter is not always possible or even desirable. For most occasions when you do get to follow your instructional plan as intended, a crucial step in the instructional cycle is reflecting on the strengths and areas you see for improvement within your lesson.

It takes time to become comfortable with reflective thinking. It is not as natural a way of thinking as you may assume at first. In order to be truly reflective of your instructional practice, you have to be open and honest with yourself. This will mean taking a hard look at your practice and asking yourself, "What did I do well today? What did I not do well? Why?" It is only natural to want to focus on what we know we did well. However, the real growth for us as teachers comes when we think critically about what we did not do so well so that we can make adjustments and improvements. While being brutally honest with yourself about your practice may feel uncomfortable at first, with time it will become a routine and vital part of your instructional cycle.

All teachers know at some level whether or not their lesson is working as they are teaching. Great teachers use this knowledge to set goals for improving their very next lesson. Goal setting is an important piece of the planning, implementing, and reflecting cycle. If we stopped after planning and implementing, then we would be ending the cycle prematurely, not having learned anything from our reflection. Taking what you learned from your reflection to set goals for improvement is also a skill that takes practice. A good goal is based on your knowledge of the best practices associated with literacy instruction and your knowledge of your students' understanding. Setting a goal requires thinking about what you can do to improve an area you identified during reflection that can be strengthened. It also requires you to think realistically about what you can accomplish in your read-aloud experience with your unique group of young students.

To help you think about how to think reflectively and to set goals as a result of your reflection, we have included case studies in each of the following chapters. The case studies provide example teacher talk during read-alouds with students at different grade levels. We describe for you what teacher talk would sound like during a read-aloud focused on each of the literacy elements, and then provide you with the internal reflective thinking the teacher may go through after his or her instruction. Each of our case study teachers thinks critically about the strengths and areas for improvement of his or her instruction and then sets goals for addressing these areas in the very next read-aloud. We have included columns for reflecting and goal setting within the planning template. Each chapter includes a completed template based on our case study teacher as an example. Again, blank planning templates are located in the Appendix for your own use.

Final Thoughts

The remainder of this book is devoted to helping you create read-alouds that incorporate best practices in literacy instruction for young students. Each chapter summarizes research-based instructional activities for teaching one of the literacy elements described in the preface: oral language, vocabulary, book and print conventions, alphabet awareness, phonological awareness, and comprehension. Within each chapter you will also find examples of how to implement the literacy activities described. A case study describes how an example teacher would go about the planning, implementing, and reflecting cycle to thoroughly develop his or her instruction of the target element. Included in each chapter is a completed planning template that the teacher would use to plan, reflect, and set goals for improvement.

We made the conscious decision to separate each literacy element into its own chapter with the knowledge that in a single read-aloud you may wish to target more than one element at a time. We have saved our discussion of combining key literacy targets in the same reading for our last chapter, which considers tracking your progress with literacy instruction over time. In the final chapter we also discuss knowing where to begin your literacy instruction and the benefits of repeated reading.

The following chapters are presented in no particular order. All of the literacy elements targeted for this book are important components of an overall literacy program for young students and should be introduced and taught hand in hand. As you consider how to implement the best practices identified for each of the target literacy elements, remember the great instructional opportunity read-alouds offer for developing both the foundational skills necessary for young readers and the lifelong joy of reading. We hope you will come to believe in the power of the read-aloud as much as we have.

CHAPTER 3

Developing Oral Language through Read-Alouds

Let's talk! Children who hear a lot of talk and who are encouraged to talk themselves are provided with a solid foundation for learning how to read (Armbruster, Lehr, & Osborn, 2003). Through conversations with parents, caregivers, teachers, and peers, children gain valuable oral language skills that they will apply throughout their academic career and lives. Consequently, teachers of young children play an important role in providing opportunities to bolster and boost children's oral language development. Read-alouds can be playfully and purposefully planned to accomplish that goal.

Planning the Reading

The planning portion of your read-aloud sets the tone for the actual implementation of your read-aloud time. It's the foundation of a successful read-aloud experience. Once you have a plan, you'll begin your read-aloud time with a focus, goals, and a vision of where you'd like to take your students during this wonderful literacy and language experience. Planning to target oral language development in read-alouds involves careful consideration of the skill, the text, and the instructional strategies that will target the skill. Since oral language development is focused on increasing the amount of talk, teachers must plan for multiple opportunities to model rich language and involve children in extended conversations surrounding the book with both the teacher and with peers. Once the target skill is chosen, teachers must also consider the type of book that is best suited to meet that objective.

Matching a Book to the Skill

Effective read-alouds provide opportunities for interactions with great books. Ultimately, all children's books offer some sort of opportunity for discussion. However, books that are built and designed to elicit rich talk and adult–child conversations share some similar characteristics.

We provide you with some considerations on those characteristics and on the selection of books that could heighten the level of literary and discussions on fiction and nonfiction books with your students. First, look for books that are filled with rich language and vocabulary. You should be able to find lots of descriptive passages and interesting vocabulary sprinkled throughout the selection. Children's books contain many words that children are unlikely to encounter frequently in their daily conversations. Read-alouds provide the perfect time for children to hear and use these words and ultimately add these words to their oral language repertoires. Books should also contain plenty of examples of beautiful and captivating artwork. Consider the discussions that you can initiate with your children about these wonderful illustrations.

Second, be thoughtful about the book's story line. The story line and plot should be original and filled with lots of opportunities for children to discuss the interesting twists and turns of the plot. Along with the story line, consider the characters in the book. The character or characters should be engaging, interesting, and entertaining. The characters should be round, rather than flat. In other words, the characters themselves should undergo a transformation during the events of the story, and these changes provide for many opportunities for discussion and reflection. Last, if you are reading a nonfiction selection, choose books that are about interesting topics and are filled with real-life photographs and descriptions. Young children truly love nonfiction books, and they provide for limitless opportunities for exciting discussions and wonderment. See Figure 3.1 for a quick reference of considerations when

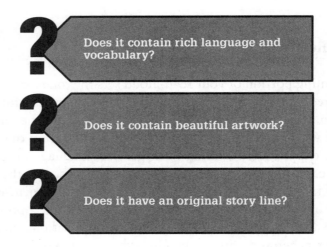

FIGURE 3.1. Considerations for choosing books that build oral language.

choosing texts ideal for boosting children's oral language. In the process of making a book selection ask yourself the question "Do I think that my children will want to revisit this text over and over again?" If your answer is "yes," then you know you made a successful selection. We know that children who are provided with repeated readings of one book tend to grow their language, vocabulary, and comprehension development. They also tend to grow their love of literacy—and that is a positive thing for their academic growth.

You may likely find that you already have many selections in your classroom library collection that contain these outlined characteristics. They may have been read alouds that you have traditionally read each and every year when teaching a specific theme or concept. We ask that you take another look at these selections. Take a closer examination to find their potential to offer opportunities to build children's oral language. For example, you may read the favorite children's books *The Mitten* by Jan Brett (1997), *The Snowman* by Raymond Briggs (1978), or *The Snowy Day* by Ezra Jack Keats (1962) as a regular part of your "winter" theme every year. They are all certainly perfectly wonderful books that directly connect to the concept of wintertime. However, not only do these selections exemplify the theme but they also provide a plethora of opportunities to increase the amount of talk in your read-aloud time. In addition to the selections on your shelves that we hope you "rediscover" as ideal to build children's oral language, we have provided you with a list of both fiction and nonfiction that you might also consider adding to your shelves in Figure 3.2.

Deciding How to Develop the Skill

So now that you have planned to target oral language development in your read-aloud and chosen the perfect book, you're ready to focus on the best practices that you can implement to develop that skill. The read-aloud is the ideal time to target oral language development through increased amount of talk. In the next section, we've provided some research-based strategies to assist you in accomplishing that goal.

The first thing you want to keep in mind is that in your reading you should consistently model rich and robust language surrounding the read-aloud. So, the first strategy to plan for is to *model rich language* (e.g., Wasik & Bond, 2001). This requires you to intersperse rich language before, during, and after the read-aloud. It involves adding an ongoing commentary to the story. So, in addition to reading the words in the text, stop and describe what is happening so far in the story, describe what is happening in the pictures, or ask questions about what you think might happen next. In this sense, you are thinking aloud all of the thoughts that you as a competent reader have about what is happening in the text. As you are modeling this rich language, you allow the children to hear your thoughts, provide them the insight that reading is thinking, expand their listening, or receptive language, and most powerfully, to enjoy the opportunity to verbalize their own thoughts and ideas.

Fiction Selections	Nonfiction Selections
Bad Kitty by Nick Bruel (2005)	*Ice Cream: The Full Scoop* by Gail Gibbons (2008)
The Old Woman Who Named Things by Cynthia Rylant (2000)	*Spiders* by Seymour Simon (2007)
Odd Velvet by Mary E. Whitcomb (1998)	*Caves* by Stephen P. Kramer (1995)
Chocolatina by Erik Kraft (2008)	*This Is the Way We Go to School* by Laine Falk (2009)
Alexander and the Terrible, Horrible, No Good, Very Bad Day by Judith Viorst (2009)	*Pumpkin Circle: The Story of a Garden* by George Levenson (2002)
Corduroy by Don Freeman (1968)	*Is It a Living Thing?* by Bobbie Kalman (2007)
Officer Buckle and Gloria by Peggy Rathman (1995)	*Red Leaf, Yellow Leaf* by Lois Ehlert (1991)
Enemy Pie by Derek Munson (2000)	*What Do You Do with a Tail Like This?* (Caldecott Honor Book) by Steve Jenkins (2003)
Imogene's Antlers by David Small (1989)	*Jack's Garden* by Henry Cole (1997)
Brave Irene by William Steig (1988)	*Whose Hat Is This?* by Katz Cooper (2007)
The Paper Bag Princess by Robert Munsch (1992)	*A Log's Life* by Wendy Pfeffer (2007)
A Chair for My Mother (Caldecott Honor Book) by Vera B. Williams (1984)	*Under One Rock: Bug, Slugs, and Other Ughs* by Anthony Fredericks (2001)
Owl Moon (Caldecott Medal) by Jane Yolen (1987)	*Pop! A Book about Bubbles* by Kimberly Bradley (2001)
Come On, Rain! by Karen Hesse (1999)	*What Is a Scientist?* by Barbara Lehn (1999)
Peter's Chair by Ezra Jack Keats (1998)	*Look How It Changes!* by June Young (2006)

FIGURE 3.2. Books on our shelves to build oral language development.

This, of course, leads us to the next strategy, which includes *asking open-ended questions* (e.g., Justice, Weber, Ezell, & Bakeman, 2002; Neuman & Celano, 2001; Neuman, Copple, & Bredekamp, 2000). You should plan to ask several open-ended questions in the before, during, and after stages of the read-aloud. While closed questions only allow for a one- or two-word response, open-ended questions allow for a multitude of responses and allow children the opportunity to expand their oral language and vocabulary. So, questions that begin with "How?" or "Why?" are typically those that allow individualized thoughts and ideas from children. A great way to make the most out of asking open-ended questions is to have your children engage in the *turn-and-talk strategy*. This allows each and every child in the class the opportunity to expand his or her oral language. For example, a teacher might ask, "How do you think he feels about starting his first day of school? I want you to turn and talk. Whisper to your partner how you think he might feel about starting his first day of school." In this way, each child is able to participate, and in this case, expand his or her oral language, and some children might also share their ideas with the group.

The next two strategies that also link very well to asking open-ended questions is providing *language repetition and expansion* and providing *language follow-up prompts* (e.g., Whitehurst et al., 1994). These are strategies that teachers are ready to use during those times in read-alouds when the focus is all about increasing the amount of talk and holding the children accountable for raising the level of talk. So, let's say that the teacher has asked a perfectly wonderful open-ended question, and a child responds with a one- or two-word answer. Do you then go to the next child, or do you push a bit further to get a more elaborated response? You've now come to the point during your reading when you need to take action and respond to children in a way that is still focused on the goal of increasing their level of discussion. If we provide our children with a little push or challenge, we are conveying that reading is thinking and discussing and that they are also held responsible for their level of participation.

Your first option is to repeat their one- or two-word answer and then expand on that answer with additional rich language and vocabulary. In this strategy, you are acting as a role model for expanding language with more thoughts and ideas. Children will begin to internalize that they can also respond to questions with more elaborated responses and they are also growing their listening, or receptive, vocabulary. Your second option releases the responsibility a bit more on the children's shoulders. This includes your providing an immediate follow-up question or prompt after a child has given a one- or two-word response. This prompt provides the child with a little help to elaborate on that short response. In both cases, teacher and children share a responsibility to expand their level of talk and discussion surrounding a read-aloud.

The final two strategies for developing oral language require teachers to be "in tune" with their children and respond to their interests, ideas, and accomplishments accordingly throughout read-aloud time; the first of which requires the teacher to take on the *role of the listener* (e.g., Hargrave & Senechal, 2000). Teachers who take on this vital role listen to children's comments and use them to engage children in conversation surrounding the story. The last strategy requires teachers to provide *praise and encouragement* during the read-aloud (e.g., Justice & Kaderavek, 2002; Wasik & Bond, 2001), which requires a shift from providing nonspecific praise to very specific praise in response to a child's behaviors. Teachers observe children's successes, participation, and approximations in regard to their level of literacy or language participation during the read-aloud and provide praise connected to those behaviors. For example, if a child responds, "I think she is excited because she is smiling and jumping up in the air," the teacher might respond, "Yes, I agree. She does look excited. I like the way you really looked at the picture to figure out how she is feeling right now and then told us all about it." In this case, the teacher responded with specific praise in response to a child's specific literacy behavior. Children then feel successful for their attempts, and this praise encourages them to reengage in that behavior in subsequent read-aloud sessions.

We have provided you with a repertoire of oral language development strategies that you can now try to begin to infuse into your very next read-aloud time. See Figure 3.3 for a quick reference to these described oral language development strategies. We hope that these strategies help you to think about your interactions with children and fills your next read-aloud time with lots of wonderful talk.

Model rich language	Intersperse descriptive language while reading story.
Ask open-ended questions	Pose open-ended questions throughout the reading. These questions begin with "How?" or "Why?"
Repeat and expand children's responses	Repeat children's responses and expand on them with rich language.
Provide follow-up prompts	Provide a follow-up question or prompt after children's initial one- or two-word responses that requires them to expand their oral language.
Be an active listener	Listen to your students' comments and ideas about the story and use them to engage students in additional conversation.
Provide specific praise and encouragement	Provide children with praise that is specific to a positive behavior they displayed (literacy or language) in storybook reading.

FIGURE 3.3. Read-aloud targets for oral language development.

Planning Template

We have created the template presented in Figure 3.4 to guide your thinking about oral language development instruction during read-alouds. A blank version of the template is available in the Appendix (Form 1). The template is divided into three columns: planning, reflecting, and goal setting. The template includes each of the outlined oral language strategies discussed in the previous section in the left-hand column and provides additional space for planning a read-aloud time that targets oral language development strategies, reflecting on the success of the oral language development instruction implemented during the read-aloud, and finally, setting goals for improving oral language development instruction for your very next read-aloud time.

In order to illustrate the use of the template, which is designed for oral language development, we follow Mrs. French, a prekindergarten teacher, in her attempts to plan, target, reflect, and set goals for oral language development in her read-aloud in the remaining sections of this chapter. Mrs. French teaches approximately 18–20 4-year-old children from a range of socioeconomic backgrounds in a church-based preschool setting. The preschool uses a prekindergarten literacy and math core curriculum. Mrs. French's typical classroom instruction includes two read-aloud times: one during morning circle meeting and the second during snack time. The classroom core curriculum emphasizes the importance of young children's oral language development and the role that it will play when they enter kindergarten. Mrs. French has decided to focus on her read-aloud time as a means to develop her oral language development strategies and ultimately increase the level of adult and child participation.

While planning for the next unit on "Me, My Family, and Friends," Mrs. French chooses the book *The Hello, Goodbye Window* by Norton Juster (2005) for her read-aloud time. The story is about a young girl and her special relationship with her grandparents, which is witnessed through what she calls "the hello, goodbye

A Focus on Oral Language Development in Read-Alouds

	Planning What is my plan?	Reflecting How did I do?	Goal Setting What will I do next time?
Rich Language Modeled	• Describe the scene on the cover of the book in great detail and connect it to the title. • Stop and discuss all of the events that take place in the kitchen and connect these ideas to *The Hello, Goodbye Window*.		
Open-Ended Questions	• Why is the window so special for the little girl? • Do you think that she is really seeing all of those things in the window? Why? • What would you like to see out of your hello, goodbye window?		
Language Repetition and Expansion	• Be ready to repeat and add a lot of detail and elaboration if students respond with a limited response after a question I pose.		
Language Follow-Up Prompts	• Be ready to ask a follow-up question if students can't respond or give a limited response. Help them to elaborate on their initial response.		
Role of Listener	• I imagine that my students will comment on the pictures and the events surrounding the window. Listen and ask them questions about their comments and wonderment.		
Praise and Encouragement	• If I observe specific language behaviors, I will praise and encourage these behaviors.		

FIGURE 3.4. Mrs. French's initial planning template.

window." Mrs. French chose this book for several reasons. First, the book connects very nicely to the theme of my family and me. Second, she notes that the book has been awarded the Caldecott Medal, and she does notice the beautiful illustrations. She also pages through the book and finds lots of descriptive passages and words that she knows would be wonderful to introduce into her children's vocabulary. She finds the characters quite unique and interesting, and the story line is one that she has never come across before. She believes that her children will be drawn to the illustrations and will find many personal connections to the character and story line.

Now that Mrs. French has chosen the read-aloud selection, she starts to plan how she will implement her read-aloud. She uses the planning section of the template and the outlined best practices on the template to do this. The first best practice is to model rich language. Mrs. French looks at the picture on the front cover and decides that she will provide a rich description of the scene and connect this description to the title *The Hello, Goodbye Window* (Juster, 2005). As she reads through the book several times to gain familiarity with the book, she takes note of the significance of the window being in the kitchen and the specific events that occur in the kitchen and how they are connected to the window. She decides that she will stop at several spots and use the rich language and vocabulary in the book to connect the kitchen and the window. This modeling of rich language by providing a think-aloud commentary supports the children in their attempts to answer open-ended questions. She composes three open-ended questions on sticky notes and places them on the pages where she will ask those questions. She likes this idea because she often forgets to ask certain questions during read-alouds. She is careful to come up with questions that begin with "Why?" and "How?" and "Do you?" She imagines that this will provide an opportunity for individual thoughts, ideas, and discussion. For two of the questions, she will also add the "turn-and-talk" strategy so that all children will have time to practice and expand their oral language.

The next two strategies, language repetition and expansion and language follow-up prompts are areas that Mrs. French has to be ready to implement after she has asked the open-ended questions. These are two strategies that teachers use in response to children's response. So, she notes in her planning template to be ready to repeat and expand with rich oral language and to provide a follow-up question or prompt if given a short, or one- or two-word response. The fifth strategy requires Mrs. French to be an active listener. She truly wants to add this strategy to her repertoire. She wants to model being an active listener so that her students will also become active listeners. This is crucial in developing children's oral language skills. She notes on her template that she will actively listen to her children's comments about the pictures, the characters, the window, and the events, and prompt or question her children about those comments to engage them in interesting and personal discussions. The sixth and final strategy, providing specific praise and encouragement, is a departure from her traditional, more nonspecific praise. While she will still continue to give behavior and classroom management praise, she notes that she needs to devote conscious attention to praising specific language behaviors that she wants her children to continue to use in future read-aloud sessions.

In Figure 3.4, Mrs. French has completed the planning column of the template. She has taken the time to plan the specific spots in the book where she will pause to engage in oral language development strategies. She also notes that she needs to be prepared and ready to respond specifically to children's responses. The next step is for Mrs. French to put her plan into action in her prekindergarten classroom. In the next section, we hear some of the sample talk as Mrs. French infuses oral language development strategies into her read-aloud time.

Implementing the Reading

Weaving oral language development strategies into a read-aloud does require some planning but the rewards are incredible. Teachers must be alert and prepared to respond to children in ways that encourage them to delve a little deeper and elaborate their thoughts and ideas. The desired goal is to increase the amount of talk—on behalf of the teacher and the students. We have seen Mrs. French plan a read-aloud for *The Hello, Goodbye Window* (Juster, 2005); below we describe what Mrs. French's read-aloud might sound like in the classroom.

Teacher Talk during Read-Alouds

Mrs. French completes the morning calendar routine and has her children stand up and march around the circle for their "Marching Around the Alphabet Song" that not only helps with alphabet awareness but helps her 4-year-olds get their wiggles out so they are ready for read-aloud time. Once they are sitting with "five things ready," she begins read-aloud time. Holding up the book so it is in plain view for the children and pointing to the front cover, she begins: *"Today we will be reading a new story called **The Hello, Goodbye Window**. The author is Norton Juster, and the illustrator is Chris Raschka. I notice that the book has a special gold sticker called a seal. This is an award called the Caldecott Medal, and it is given to a book if it has beautiful pictures. We will need to look very closely at the pictures on the cover and inside the book and talk about them as we read the story. I'm looking at the cover and I see a little girl waving to two people at the window and they are also waving back to her. I wonder who she is waving to? She looks very excited to see them and they also look happy to see her. I also remember that the title of the story is **The Hello, Goodbye Window**. I'm wondering if this **is** the hello, goodbye window. We will need to read to find out. Does anyone else notice anything about the picture on the cover?"* Mrs. French allows several children to provide things that they notice about the picture on the cover and uses these ideas to help children make predictions about the story.

Mrs. French begins to read the story with excitement and expression, and she and the children quickly find answers to two of their original predictions: the people in the window were her Nanny and Poppy and they were waving at each other at the hello, goodbye window. Mrs. French continues to read the story that describes the hello, goodbye window as being in the kitchen and all of the things the little girl, her Nanny, and her Poppy do out of the window. At this point, Mrs. French pauses to discuss some of these events in a little more detail and connects them to the window: *"Wow. We have found out quite a bit about the hello, goodbye window. We found out that the little girl really enjoys playing fun games with her Nanny and Poppy like peek-a-boo and tapping on the glass outside the window and hiding, and making silly faces at each other through the window. They even look at their reflections in the window at night and pretend that it's a mirror, and her Poppy tells her to come inside for dinner even though she is standing right next to him. When I think about all of those things I think about family, love, and the special memories that she is creating with her Nanny and Poppy. I think that she will always have wonderful memories about her family and the window."*

Mrs. French reads on as the book describes even more special events connected to the window. At this point she pauses and asks, *"Why do you think the window is special to the little girl?"* She pauses to let the children think. Several children raise their hand and Mrs. French calls on Cameron. *"Okay, Cameron, why do you think the window is special to the little girl?"* Cameron responds, *"She always likes the window."* Mrs. French responds, *"Yes, she does always seem to like that window. How do you know? Can you tell me a time that in the story that she seems to like the window?"* Cameron responds, *"When she and her Nanny count the stars at night."* Mrs. French responds, *"Excellent! You remembered the little girl counting the stars at night out of the window with her Nanny. I like how you thought about something that happened in the window from the story."* Mrs. French calls on two other students to respond and provides additional language follow-up prompts and specific praise and encouragement for their responses.

Mrs. French reads on and notices her children begin to talk and discuss the pictures on the page where the little girl pretends that the hello, goodbye window is a magic window. She pauses after reading that page and asks, *"What are you noticing about what is happening on this page? What are you noticing about the pictures? Turn and talk to your neighbor. Whisper in his or her ear and tell him or her what you are noticing."* She pauses to let them turn and talk. She then asks children to talk about what they were discussing with each other. Chloe responds, *"She saw a tyrannosaurus rex in the window! She can't see that. That's not real anymore!"* Mrs. French responds, *"You're right, Chloe. They are extinct. That means that they don't live anymore but that they used to a long time ago. Why do you think she might have seen a T-rex in the window?"* Several children raise their hands and Mrs. French calls on Joey. *"Joey, why do you think she sees a T-rex?"* and Joey responds, *"I think she was having a dream."* Mrs. French responds, *"Maybe you're right. She could have been daydreaming. That's when you might sit and think about all kinds of things. I think she might have also been using her imagination. What's an imagination?* Sarah raises her hands and says, *"That's when you make things up."* Mrs. French responds, *"Yes, you use your mind to create a picture. Maybe her imagination let her see a T-rex in the window."*

Mrs. French completes the story and ends with a final open-ended question: *"What would you like to see out of your hello, goodbye window?"* Mrs. French notes that her children's eyes seem to light up when she asked that question and they were so excited to share their answers. She allows them to turn and talk and then asks several to share their answers. She took this final question as an opportunity to provide language repetition and expansion, as some children gave brief responses, and also to provide praise for thinking about what they would like to see out of their own hello, goodbye window. As an extension activity, she provided each child with a frame cut out of a house and a window and had each child draw what they would see out of their hello, goodbye window. During interactive learning centers, each child then had the chance to dictate what he or she would like to see in his or her window. Mrs. French and her assistant also took this opportunity to expand their oral language by prompting and extending their dictations during this activity.

Reflecting on the Reading

Mrs. French routinely stays after school for about an hour a few days a week to plan or to create materials for her lessons or her learning centers. She takes this opportunity to sit down and reflect on her efforts to weave oral language development strategies into her read-aloud time using *The Hello, Goodbye Window* (Juster, 2005). She goes back to the same planning template but this time completes the reflection and goal-setting columns of the template. Mrs. French is not accustomed to this type of reflective practice but feels that this may really assist her in reaching her goals to improve her interactions with her children and ultimately raise the level of talk and participation. Mrs. French's completed template is presented in Figure 3.5. We take a look at Mrs. French's reflective and goal-setting practices as she thinks about the strengths and the challenges of her read-aloud time.

Thinking about Strengths and Challenges

On the whole, Mrs. French was quite happy about her read-aloud time using *The Hello, Goodbye Window* (Juster, 2005). She felt that it went well for two main reasons. First, she felt confident about implementing the read-aloud and infusing oral language strategies because she began with a plan. She was focused and ready to respond to her children's responses and behaviors. Second, she knew that she had chosen an excellent book ideal to provide opportunities to target oral language. All of this took place, of course, in the planning stage of the read-aloud. So, from the start, Mrs. French knew that it had the potential to go very well. But now, she would take this opportunity to look at the specifics in regard to her efforts to raise the level of adult–child and peer-to-peer oral language interactions.

Mrs. French begins reflecting and goal setting for the first strategy and then moves down the template. First she thinks through *modeling rich language*. She notes that she did achieve her goal to stop and describe the scene on the cover and to stop and describe and summarize several key events surrounding the hello, goodbye window. However, she would like to plan to add more sophisticated words in her descriptions in future read-alouds. She feels that this strategy lends itself nicely to adding to her children's vocabulary. She hopes that by modeling this rich language, her children will begin to use these words themselves. Next, she thinks about the *open-ended questions* she asked and her children's responses to these questions. Several reflections spring to her mind regarding this strategy. She notes that she did ask these questions, and having the sticky notes in the book helped to ensure that she did. She found that her more verbal children were the only ones raising their hands to answer these questions and while they provided answers that were related to the story, the answers were not well elaborated. She knows that she needs to hold all children accountable and that if she continues to call on the same few children every time, other children will be even less likely to actively participate.

She then takes up to the next two strategies, *language repetition and expansion* and *language follow-up prompts* to help her and her children achieve this goal. She realizes that both of these are critical teacher-response behaviors. She notes that she did use language follow-up prompts for those children who needed a little push in extending or elaborating their response, and this worked well. She also notes that she used language repetition and expansion to model using rich language to elaborate on a response but that she will need to use this more in future read-alouds. She feels that this will work for her children who are less verbal or who have trouble elaborating a response even after some prompting. She remembers that read-aloud time is a supportive context. She will work toward supporting all of her children's needs whether that means providing an extra push by providing a prompt or by repeating and expanding on a response by modeling rich language.

The final two strategies, *role of the listener* and *provide specific praise and encouragement*, were new strategies that Mrs. French knew she needed to give conscious attention to during the read-aloud. She notes that she felt more "in tune" with her children given that she was consciously attending to their thoughts and comments during the read-aloud. She was pleasantly surprised at their reaction to the little girl looking out of the window and using her imagination. Almost all of her class responded to this page and began to talk about the pictures. She took this unplanned opportunity to have her children "turn and talk" to one another about what they were noticing in the pictures. She knows that this was an incredible opportunity to expand all children's oral language and that she will continue to tune in to her children's thoughts and connections in future read-aloud sessions. Last, she reflects on her ability to shift her traditional praise to very specific praise targeted to an oral language behavior. She found doing this was easier than originally expected

A Focus on Oral Language Development in Read-Alouds

	Planning What is my plan?	Reflecting How did I do?	Goal Setting What will I do next time?
Rich Language Modeled	• Describe the scene on the cover of the book in great detail and connect it to the title. • Stop and discuss all of the events that take place in the kitchen and connect these ideas to *The Hello, Goodbye Window*.	• I did model rich language when I described the scene but I could have used some additional rare vocabulary words. • I discussed the events that occurred in the window. I think it supported their attempts to answer the first open-ended question.	• Continue to add a lot of rich language by describing scenes and events but add a few more sophisticated or rare words. • Continue to add a commentary and summarize events. This really supported them when responding to questions.
Open-Ended Questions	• Why is the window so special for the little girl? • Do you think that she is really seeing all of those things in the window? Why? • What would you like to see out of your hello, goodbye window?	• I did ask all of these questions. Sticky notes helped! They did well but needed some prompting to extend their ideas. • I noticed the same children were raising their hands though.	• Continue to plan for multiple open-ended questions. • Continue to use "turn and talk" and call on more children during these times.
Language Repetition and Expansion	• Be ready to repeat and add a lot of detail and elaboration if students respond with a limited response after a question I pose.	• I did this a few times. I wanted to model how to extend their responses. I need to add some more rare words.	• Continue this practice, especially for those who can't elaborate even after some prompting. • Add more rare words.
Language Follow-Up Prompts	• Be ready to ask a follow-up question if students can't respond or give a limited response. Help them to elaborate on their initial response.	• I did this as well. My more verbal children responded well to this. They just needed a little push to get there.	• Continue this practice for all children. I think this will take some time for some but after repeating this practice, level of talk will increase.
Role of Listener	• I imagine that my students will comment on the pictures and the events surrounding the window. Listen and ask them questions about their comments and wonderment.	• Children loved the page where she was using her imagination. I listened to their comments and then used "turn and talk" for them to share.	• Continue to "tune in" to my children. It may just lead to unplanned oral language opportunities!
Praise and Encouragement	• If I observe specific language behaviors, I will praise and encourage these behaviors.	• This was a change for me but I tried to give praise for specific language behaviors.	• Continue because children will repeat those behaviors.

FIGURE 3.5. Mrs. French's completed template.

and could be accomplished by tailoring her response to children's responses and behaviors throughout the read-aloud. If they responded to a question, she praised them for really thinking about what happened in the story or really looking at the pictures to tell what the story might be about. When her students all "turned and talked," she praised everyone for talking about what they thought or what they were noticing in the story. She plans to continue this strategy in the hope that more and more of her children will adopt these language behaviors in future read-alouds.

Closing Thoughts

Infusing oral language development strategies into your read-alouds provide the perfect context to boost children's oral language development. The focus of read-alouds that target oral language is to increase the amount of talk that children both hear and use. Read-aloud selections that are ideal for this purpose contain rich language and vocabulary, beautiful artwork, captivating characters and story lines, and interesting and real-world topics. We provided six research-based practices that will help you to focus on increasing the level of participation that include (1) modeling rich language, (2) asking open-ended questions, (3) providing language repetition and expansion, (4) providing language follow-up prompts, (5) being an active listener, and (6) providing specific praise and encouragement. We also provided a template (Figure 3.4) to assist you in planning these experiences in your read-aloud as well as the opportunity to reflect and set goals for future read-alouds. A blank planning template is presented in the Appendix for you to use to plan, reflect, and set goals for targeting oral language development in your future read-alouds.

CHAPTER 4

Developing Vocabulary through Read-Alouds

Wonderful words make a difference! Children who have been exposed to rich and robust language experiences filled with wonderful words enter school with essential language skills that are needed to be successful readers, whereas those who enter school having had limited exposures to rich vocabulary tend to struggle with reading as they move through their school career (Hirsch, 2006). Consequently, teachers of young children play an important role in planning experiences that will grow children's vocabulary. Read-alouds provide the perfect context to target those wonderful words and grow children's vocabulary each and every day.

Planning the Reading

Planning to target vocabulary in your read-alouds involves careful consideration of the skill, the text, and the instructional strategies designed to target the skill. A read-aloud that focuses on vocabulary involves rich discussions and conversations about specific vocabulary words within the book. These discussions about the targeted words occur before, during, and after reading. Once you have decided to focus on vocabulary instruction, you must also consider the type of book that is ideal to accomplish that goal.

Matching a Book to the Skill

Children's books are positively brimming with wonderful words to target and teach. It is interesting to note that children's literature contains more rare words than children hear or use in conversations in their daily lives. The language of children's books is unique because they contain words and ideas that are outside of the here and now (Adams, 1990). This kind of language is called decontextualized language. As early childhood educators, we need to identify these words within the books and make them accessible to children so that these words will live within their lives. The first step in this process is to locate books that will offer these critical language development opportunities.

Children's books that are designed to grow children's vocabulary are chocka-block (filled with) magnificent words. So what are magnificent words? Beck and McKeown (2007) call them Tier Two words. Tier Two words are those "just right" words: not too hard and not too easy. They are high-frequency words that are unfamiliar to your children but are those that they will find useful and interesting in their own lives and across all academic areas of instruction. See Figure 4.1 for a description of Beck and McKeown's tiered words. We need to closely examine the books that we read to our children and identify whether the book does indeed contain words that will be useful to target and teach. Let's talk about some specific considerations when choosing books that build children's vocabulary knowledge.

You'll notice that many of the considerations for books that build oral language are also ideal for building children's vocabulary. Instructionally this can be considered to be a blessing as it is quite easy to target both oral language and vocabulary in one read-aloud session. (We discuss overlapping target areas in one reading in the Chapter 9.) First and foremost, you should be able to locate several examples of Tier Two words within the book. These words will ultimately serve as the basis for a targeted vocabulary discussion before, during, and after the reading. Remember the questions to ask yourself when thinking about specific words to target. These include, "Is the word unfamiliar to a majority of my children?" "Will they find the

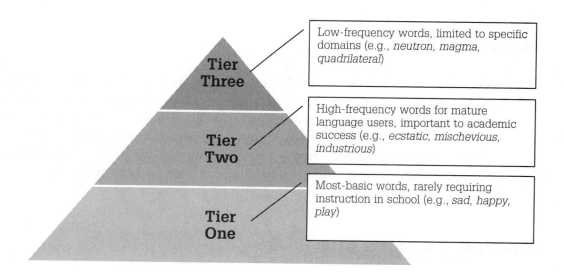

FIGURE 4.1. Tier word categories. Based on Beck, McKeown, and Kucan (2002).

word interesting?" and "Will this word be useful in their lives?" See Figure 4.2 for a quick reference guide for selecting those spectacular words.

Second, the book should contain lots of examples of captivating illustrations. These illustrations may serve as a medium to discuss the words that you have chosen to target and discuss. For example, if you have targeted the word *curious*, you can find an illustration in the book that shows a character acting *curious*. Next, the book should contain interesting characters and original story lines. This also serves as a powerful medium to discuss those words that you have targeted to teach. The characters and the plot can easily be weaved into your discussion about those words because of the interconnectedness of the content of the book and the words chosen to write the story. For example, if you target the word *fortunate*, you can discuss how the main character was fortunate in the story as a part of your discussion surrounding the word *fortunate*. Finally, the book should be one that you can envision your children wanting to hear several times. Why is this important? Research has found that children who have had multiple readings of one book have increased their comprehension of the story as well as their number of novel (new) vocabulary words gained from having had the book read aloud (e.g., Elley, 1989). Figure 4.3 lists criteria for choosing books to build children's vocabulary knowledge.

The good news is that you most likely have many selections in your classroom library that meet these criteria. You might find that your favorite read-aloud selections that you use time and time again to connect to your themes or curriculum content standards contain a plethora of wonderful words. We ask that you take another look at these selections and "rediscover" them for their vocabulary development potential. On the other hand, after having examined these books, you might find that they have a dearth of wonderful words. You might decide that a book no longer meets the guidelines for developing your children's vocabulary knowledge. Nevertheless, this book may be used for the development of other skills necessary for literacy. Therefore, we do not suggest you get rid of books that do not have

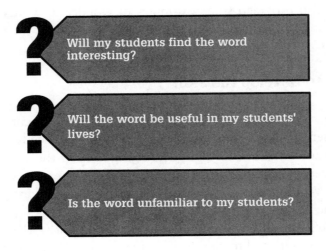

Will my students find the word interesting?

Will the word be useful in my students' lives?

Is the word unfamiliar to my students?

FIGURE 4.2. Considerations for choosing wonderful words.

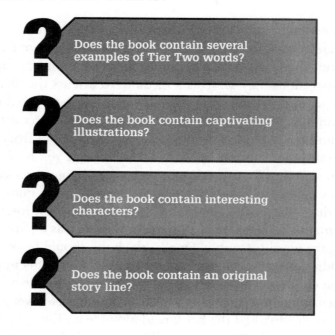

FIGURE 4.3. Criteria for choosing books to build vocabulary.

these specific characteristics but rather that you consciously judge the effectiveness of these books in your instruction. If you find that they do not serve the needs of your instructional goals, it is better to remove them from your library. The main idea is that you act as the gateway for deciding what constitutes high-quality children's literature. Be sure to ask yourself, "Does this book contain wonderful words that I want to introduce into my children's vocabulary?" In addition to the selections on your shelves that are ideal to build your children's vocabulary, we have provided you with a list of books that contain an abundance of fabulous words in Figure 4.4. We have also provided some examples of wonderful words (Tier Two words) that can be found in each selection.

Deciding How to Develop the Skill

After you have planned to target vocabulary development in your read-aloud and have chosen the book you think that addresses the needs of your instruction, you now need to focus on how you're going to develop the skill. It's important to consider the best practices that you will weave into your read-aloud that will build your children's vocabulary. In the next section, we provide key research-based practices to help you accomplish that goal.

The first thing that you'll need to do is to identify the specific words to target and teach. You'll need to closely examine the words in the selection and choose one to three specific Tier Two words that meet the guidelines previously discussed as

Selection	Sample Wonderful Words
Brave Irene by William Steig (1986)	<ul><li>*brave*</li><li>*clutching*</li><li>*coaxed*</li><li>*radiant*</li></ul>
A Pocket for Corduroy by Don Freeman (1978)	<ul><li>reluctant</li><li>*drowsy*</li><li>*insisted*</li></ul>
Sylvester and the Magic Pebble by William Steig (2005)	<ul><li>*inquiring*</li><li>*miserable*</li><li>*remarkable*</li><li>*usual*</li></ul>
The Mitten by Jan Brett (1997)	<ul><li>*commotion*</li><li>*investigate*</li><li>*admire*</li></ul>
Sweet Dream Pie by Audrey Wood (2002)	<ul><li>*enormous*</li><li>*thrilled*</li><li>*dismay*</li></ul>
A Bad Case of Stripes by David Shannon (1998)	<ul><li>*impress*</li><li>*relieved*</li><li>*distraction*</li></ul>
The Grannyman by Judith Byron Schachner (1999)	<ul><li>*adored*</li><li>*irresistible*</li><li>*imitate*</li></ul>
Wolf! by Becky Bloom (1999)	<ul><li>*emergency*</li><li>*concentrate*</li><li>*ignore*</li></ul>
Six-Dinner Sid by Inga Moore (1993)	<ul><li>*perfect*</li><li>*suspicious*</li><li>*curious*</li></ul>
Doctor De Soto by William Steig (1982)	<ul><li>*timid*</li><li>*protect*</li><li>*delicate*</li></ul>

FIGURE 4.4. Books on our shelves that build vocabulary.

being ideal words to target. The question then arises, "How many words should I teach in one read-aloud?" This truly depends on your audience. If you are working with prekindergarten children, one to two words per reading seems to work best. If you are working with kindergarten or first-grade children, two to three words per reading seems to be ideal. If you are just beginning to weave vocabulary instruction into a read-aloud, you may just want to begin with one word. After you've gained some comfort and familiarity with the strategies, you may decide to introduce two or three words per reading. The central idea here is that you meet the needs of your students while also meeting your professional development needs.

After you have selected the one to three specific words that you will target and teach, you'll need to consider the instructional strategies to weave into the reading to discuss these words. The vocabulary development strategies that you'll plan for occur before, during, and after the reading. The first strategy, *specific word introduction*, occurs both directly before and after you've read the story. This involves introducing the specific word or words using a picture card with the word under the picture or the use of a prop (Johnson & Yeates, 2006; Wasik & Bond, 2001). Before the reading, use the picture card or prop to introduce the word or words to alert your children to listen for that word while you are reading today and tell them that you will discuss the word after you have completed the read-aloud. Oftentimes, teachers ask children to give them a "thumbs-up" or to put their hands on their head when they hear the word while they are reading. This simple strategy seems to "tune their ears" for the word or words and truly fosters a sense of word consciousness—an appreciation and interest in words. After the reading, reintroduce the word using the picture card or prop again. This strategy will initiate the first step in an after-reading vocabulary instructional sequence that we discuss after the next strategy.

The next strategy, *specific word discussed during reading*, involves briefly defining the word when you come to the word as you are reading the story. This involves pausing when you come to the specific word or words and giving a quick, child-friendly definition of the word (Hargrave & Senechal, 2000; Robbins & Ehri, 1994). Child-friendly definitions are explanations of the vocabulary word that children can quickly understand and grasp. Unlike dictionary definitions, child-friendly definitions are created by the teacher using words that the particular group of children already understands and uses in their daily lives. During the reading portion, you can also take this opportunity to check and see whether your children remembered the every-pupil-response activity when they heard this word. The idea supporting this strategy is that you're pausing to discuss wonderful words found in the story (fostering word consciousness), while not detracting from the flow and plot of the story.

The next set of strategies occurs directly after the reading and follows a specific instructional sequence. This sequence of instruction involves providing specific attention and discussion surrounding the specific word or words that you have planned to target and teach. The first step in the after-reading sequence, *specific word introduction*, involves reintroducing the picture card or prop that you had already introduced before you began reading the story. This first step in the sequence begins the targeted discussion about the word or words. At this point, the teacher simply holds up the picture card or prop and names the word by saying, "Today one of the words that we read in our story was *enormous*." The next step, *specific word repeated*, asks the children to repeat the word. Research indicates that this allows for children to "hook" that word in their memory by having the opportunity to actually verbalize the word (Beck, McKeown, & Kucan, 2002). The teacher might ask, "What word are we talking about today?" The children will then reply, "*Enormous*." The third step in the sequence, *specific word in child-friendly terms*, requires you to provide a child-friendly definition of the word (Wasik, Bond, & Hindman, 2006). For example, a teacher might say, "*Enormous* means really, really big." Note that you would have already provided that child-friendly definition while you were reading and now you are providing it again in this after-reading sequence.

The fourth step, *specific word as used in the story*, requires you to physically go back into the pages of the book and read the word, for example, the word *enormous*, as it was used in the story (Beck & McKeown, 2007). For example, in the story *Officer Buckle and Gloria* by Peggy Rathmann (1995), Officer Buckle gets an enormous envelope stuffed with thank-you notes. At this point, you should go back into the story, read the page using the word *enormous*, and discuss what the word *enormous* means in the story. This underscores how the word *enormous* was used in the context of the story. Although powerful, research says it's not enough (Scott & Nagy, 2004). That's where the next step, *specific word used outside the story*, is critical. As educators, we want children to see the value and the usefulness of words in their own lives. Ultimately, we want that word to live in their personal vocabularies. After you have provided a context for the word *enormous* as used in the story, you'll need to have several examples of the word *enormous* as it can be used outside of the story. You'll need to think about these ahead of time. You might say that an elephant is enormous, a tyrannosaurus rex is enormous, or skyscrapers are enormous. In this sense, your children will understand that the word doesn't just exist in the book but that it's useful in their lives.

The final step, *specific word examples from students*, asks the children to provide their own examples of how they could use the word (Biemiller, 2001). It requires children to process the definition of the word and relate that word to something in their own lives and is often the most difficult step for young children in the sequence. This is where the concept of repeated readings becomes important. It may be that the first time that the word is introduced that children have difficulty verbalizing their own explanations of the word. You have the option of asking children to "act out" the word or show you with a look on their face what the word means. For example, if you are teaching the word *enormous*, you might ask them to show you what *enormous* might look like. Your children might open their arms up really wide or they might stand on their toes and reach as high as they can. Even though they may not have provided a verbalized example, they still are attaching meaning of the word with an action. You'll find that on the second or third reading of the book and discussing the specific word or words, that children will be far more likely to provide more well-elaborated explanations and understandings of the word.

An excellent way to end this instructional sequence is to ask the children to repeat the word or words one more time. A teacher might ask, "What's the word that we have been talking about today that means really, really big?" The children would then answer, "*Enormous*!" Note that this after-reading sequence provides children with a child-friendly definition of the word, provides context for the word in the story, outside of the story, and requests children to make personal connections to the word. This sequence represents rich and robust vocabulary instruction and helps to ensure that these words will be added to your children's overall vocabulary knowledge. It should also be noted that this after-reading instructional sequence should only take about 5–8 minutes. It should be value added rather than overtaking the read-aloud itself.

We have provided a useful vocabulary instructional sequence that you can now try to begin to weave into a read-aloud tomorrow. See Figure 4.5 for a quick reference to the outlined sequence of best practices in vocabulary instruction. We hope that this outline helps you to think about the wonderful words in your read-alouds and how you can make them come alive in your very next read-aloud.

Before the Read-Aloud

Introduce Specific Word—Show the children the picture card/prop, name the word, and ask them to listen for the word in the story.

During the Read-Aloud

1. **Infuse Specific Word into Story**—Pause when you come to specific word(s) and provide a child-friendly definition of the word.
2. **Identify Specific Word in Story**—If the specific word is a noun, ask the children to orally identify or point to the picture in the story.

After the Read-Aloud: 5–8 Minutes

1. **Introduce the Specific Word**—Use picture card or prop to introduce the specific word(s) and name the word(s).
2. **Repeat the Specific Word**—Ask the children to repeat the word(s).
3. **Provide the Specific Word Definition**—Provide a child-friendly definition of the word(s).
4. **Explain the Specific Word as Used in the Story**—Go back into the story and discuss how the word was used.
5. **Explain the Specific Word Outside of the Story**—Provide several examples/pictures/props of the specific word(s) outside the context of the story.
6. **Extend the Specific Word**—Encourage the children to explain or act out their understandings of the word(s).
7. **Repeat the Specific Word**—Ask the children to repeat the word again.

FIGURE 4.5. Best practices in vocabulary instruction.

Planning Template

We have created the template in Figure 4.6 to guide your thinking about vocabulary development instruction during read-alouds. The template includes the outlined vocabulary development sequence presented in the previous section in the left-hand column and spaces for you to plan, reflect, and set future goals for improvement. A blank version of the template is available in the Appendix (Form 2).

To illustrate the use of the template for vocabulary development, we follow Ms. Ramirez, a kindergarten teacher, in her efforts to plan, target, reflect, and set goals for vocabulary development in her read-aloud in the remaining sections of this chapter. Ms. Ramirez teaches 20 at-risk kindergarten children in a full-day public school setting. Her children have been identified as at risk based on their income level as well as math and literacy assessment results. Most of her children have had no previous preschool experiences and have limited literacy and language exposures prior to entering her kindergarten classroom. The school provides a healthy dose of literacy and language interventions for these children on a weekly basis. A speech–language pathologist provides three language lessons per week for her entire group of children. These lessons encourage children to participate in extended language interactions with their peers and the speech–language pathologist through the use of interactive read-alouds, choral reading, puppet plays, and Readers' Theatre. A reading specialist also provides two lessons per week for her entire group of children focusing on literacy skills such as letter identification, phonological awareness, and concepts of print.

The school is making every effort to provide these children with the critical literacy and language skills that they will need to be successful readers. Ms. Ramirez also makes every effort to do her part. She is aware that her children entered her classroom with severe deficits in language and vocabulary exposures. She also knows the powerful role that read-aloud plays in building and growing her children's language and vocabulary but wants to ensure that she is using best practices in vocabulary instruction. She has decided to focus her read-aloud time as a means to develop her vocabulary development strategies and ultimately, bolster her children's vocabulary knowledge.

While planning for the next unit on the winter theme, Ms. Ramirez decided to rename it as the "Wonderful Winter Wonderland" theme to really start to focus her children's attention on "wonderful words" all around them in an effort to develop their word consciousness and grow their vocabulary. Ms. Ramirez has several selections that she typically reads during the winter theme and now takes this opportunity to take a closer look at those books to see if she can find those wonderful words that she wants her children to add to their "vocabulary stores. She peruses the books and finds several examples of sophisticated words that she can weave into her read-aloud instruction. She is also excited to add a new book, *Brave Irene* by William Steig (1986), to her winter read-aloud selections. This story is about a girl named Irene who shows bravery and courage in the face of adversity. Her mother, a

A Focus on Vocabulary in Read-Alouds

	Planning What is my plan?	Reflecting How did I do?	Goal Setting What will I do next time?
Vocabulary Introduction (before and after reading)	brave and clutch brave: picture/word card with a firefighter going into burning building. clutch: picture/word card with a Mom holding her child's hand as they cross the street. Ask children to listen for the word in story (touch their ears).		
Vocabulary Infused into Storybook (during reading)	Pause when I come to the words in the story. Brave means to do something even if you might be scared and Clutch means to hold onto to something very tightly. Check to see if children listened and touched their ears.		
Vocabulary Repeated (after reading)	After I introduce picture cards again and say the words, I will ask children to repeat the words brave and clutch.		
Vocabulary in Child-Friendly Terms (after reading)	After the children repeat the words, I will give them the child-friendly definitions of the words (same as the ones I gave during the reading).		
Vocabulary Contextualized (after reading)	Go back into the pages of the book and discuss how the words were used: Irene was brave when she took the dress to the duchess in the snowstorm and Irene clutched the box with the dress so she wouldn't drop it in the snow and the wind.		
Vocabulary in Other Contexts (after reading)	You are brave if you get a shot at the doctor's even though it might hurt or you're brave when you first learn how to ride a bike without training wheels. You might clutch your parent's hand when you cross the street or you might clutch your teddy bear when you sleep at night.		
Vocabulary Extended (after reading)	Ask children to give examples of the words: Is there a time when you had to be brave? Have you ever clutched anything? Can you show me how to clutch this baseball bat?		

FIGURE 4.6. Ms. Ramirez's initial planning template.

dressmaker, has fallen ill and can't deliver a dress to the duchess for the grand ball that evening. Irene decides to deliver the dress for her mother and must walk for miles through a terrible snowstorm to reach her destination. Ms. Ramirez thinks that this is the perfect book. It connects to the winter theme and has a plethora of wonderful words that she can discuss with her children. It also has a brave and courageous main character and a heartwarming story line.

Now that Ms. Ramirez has chosen the book, she starts to plan how she will go about weaving vocabulary instruction into her read-aloud. She is glad that she has a planning template that provides best practices in vocabulary instruction. She wants to ensure that she makes the most out of this ideal time. She works through each step of the best practices on the planning template in succession. The first strategy is to introduce the specific word or words before and after the reading by using a picture card with the word written under the picture or through the use of a prop. She has chosen two words: *brave* and *clutching*. She chose these words after considering if the words would be useful in her children's lives, if the words would be interesting to her children, if she could imagine her children saying and using these words in many contexts, and if the words were relatively unfamiliar to her children. She also finds that the words will also connect well to the theme and discussion surrounding the story. She plans to make picture cards for each word. The word *brave* will be represented by a firefighter going into a burning building, and the word *clutching* will be represented by a child holding onto a mother's hand while crossing a busy street. Before reading the story, she plans to introduce the words by using the picture cards and will ask the children to touch their ears when they hear the words *brave* and *clutching* while she is reading the story. She also plans to use the picture cards again right after the reading to begin the after reading vocabulary sequence of instruction.

The next strategy is to provide a child-friendly definition of the specific words during the reading. Ms. Ramirez plans to pause briefly while she is reading *Brave Irene* (Steig, 1986) to give quick definitions of the words that her children will immediately understand and grasp. She takes this time to create child-friendly definitions. She defines *brave* as doing something even if you might be a little scared, and she defines *clutching* as holding onto something really tight. She also makes a note to check to see whether her children give their ears a tug when they hear these words in the story. She knows that they will be excited to listen for these words.

The final strategies occur in a sequence of instruction directly after the reading. Ms. Ramirez notes that she will follow the sequence separately for each of the words: *brave* first and then *clutching*. The first step in the sequence is to say the word while reintroducing using the picture card or prop. She plans to reintroduce the picture cards representing the words *brave* and *clutching* to begin the after-reading discussion. The next step is to have the children repeat the words *brave* and *clutching* right after she says the word in an effort to help them remember the words long after read-aloud time has ended. After her children have repeated the word, she will provide the same quick, child-friendly definition of the words that she gave while she was reading the story. This level of repetition will be helpful for her children to understand the meaning of the words. Next, she plans to physically go back into the story and explain how each word was used in *Brave Irene* (Steig, 1986). She plans to read the sentence in which each word was used and discuss the contextualized meaning of the words *brave* and *clutching*. Next, she plans two real-world examples of how children can consider the use of the words outside the context of the story. She feels that this strategy will support them in their attempts in the final step to provide their own examples of how the word could be used in their lives. She plans a prompt for each word to probe her students' understandings of how the word could apply to them in their life experiences. Finally, she plans to ask them to repeat the word after she completes the after-reading instructional sequence.

In Figure 4.6, Ms. Ramirez has completed the planning section of the template. She has taken this time to plan the before, during, and after-reading vocabulary strategies that she will infuse into her read-aloud of *Brave Irene* (Steig, 1986). The next step is for Ms. Ramirez to implement this plan in her kindergarten classroom. In the next section, we hear some of the sample talk as she weaves vocabulary development strategies into her read-aloud time.

Implementing the Reading

Teachers need to consider the type of book that lends itself to vocabulary development, if there are wonderful words that can be drawn out and discussed, and ways to make the words accessible and real to children so that they too will find the words useful and interesting in their own lives. We have seen Ms. Ramirez plan a read-aloud for *Brave Irene* (Steig, 1986); below we provide a snapshot of what her vocabulary instructional of one of the words she selected within the read-aloud might sound like in the classroom.

Teacher Talk during Read-Alouds

Ms. Ramirez completes her morning circle meeting routines and has the children sit on the carpet for the read-aloud. First, she reviews some things that they have learned so far about winter. She has them look around the room for clues—their "Wonderful Winter Wonderland." Children are excited to talk about winter facts and the winter stories they have read so far. She then reminds them about the two enormous blizzards that they had last winter. They discuss these events, and she tells them that they are going to read a new story today called *Brave Irene* about a little girl who needed to walk for miles in a snowstorm for a very important reason. She reads the title and the name of author and the illustrator, and they make predictions about the story based on the title and the picture on the front cover.

Ms. Ramirez then begins her vocabulary instruction by setting a purpose for today's reading. Before she begins reading she tells the children, "*We are going to be talking about two wonderful words today. The first word is* **brave**." Ms. Ramirez shows the children the picture card representing the word *brave*. "*The second word we will talk about is the word clutching.*" Ms. Ramirez shows them the picture card representing the word *clutching*. She then holds them both up and says, "*I want you to listen for these two words. Listen for brave and clutching. When you hear these words I want you to touch your ears. Let's see who can be excellent listeners today.*" She then begins with the title of the story again and reads the title. "*The title of our story is called Brave Irene.*" Ms. Ramirez looks at her children and finds that most of them are touching their ears. She pauses and says, "*Excellent listeners! One of our words is right in the title. Brave means that you do something even if you might be a little scared.*" Ms. Ramirez continues reading the story and pauses when she comes to the word *clutching*. She checks to see if her children are touching their ears and says, "*Clutching means to hold onto something really tight.*"

Immediately after reading the story, she directs her children's attention back to the two wonderful words. For modeling purposes, we follow Ms. Ramirez as she completes the after-reading instructional sequence of the word *clutching*. Note that the same after-reading procedures would be followed for both words. She says, "*One of the wonderful words that we are talking about today is the word clutching. What word?*" The children all enthusiastically reply, "*Clutching*"! Ms. Ramirez then reintroduces the picture card representing the word *clutching* and provides the child-friendly definition of the word. "*Clutching means to hold something or someone really tight. I'm looking at the picture here and I see that the little girl is clutching her mother's hand as they are crossing the busy street. She is clutching her hand. She is holding it tight.*" Ms. Ramirez then says, "*We heard the word clutching in our story today, and I noticed that most of you remembered to touch your ears when we came to the word. Let's go back to that page and talk about how the word was used in the story. Here we go. It says Irene was clutching the box so the wind and the snow wouldn't carry it away. Look at Irene. She is clutching the box.*"

Ms. Ramirez then pauses and says, "*We know how Irene was clutching the box. Let me think of some ways that I might use the word clutching in my life. My little brother had a bear that he slept with every night when he was a little boy. He named it Mr. Bear. He would go to sleep clutching Mr. Bear every night. It made him feel safe and comfortable. He clutched his teddy bear. I know that when I play tug-of-war that I hold the rope very tightly. I clutch the rope so that I can pull the rope to my side.*" Then she proceeds to the next step: "*Can you think of anything that you might clutch in your life? Have you ever clutched anything at home?*" At this point, lots of hands go up and a lot of chatter begins. Ms. Ramirez says, "*Okay, Erica, tell us when you were clutching something.*" Erica states, "*I have a teddy bear and a little horse that I sleep with at night.*" Ms. Ramirez then follows up by saying, "*You have a teddy bear and a horse stuffed animal? What do you do with them when you sleep at night? Can you show me?*" Erica then acts out how she holds her stuffed animals when she goes to sleep by putting her arms around her self very tightly. Ms. Ramirez then says, "*Erica, what are you showing us?*" Erica says, "*I am holding my bear.*" Ms. Ramirez then says, "*What's the word that means holding something or someone very tightly?*" Erica then provides the word: "*Clutching*"!

Ms. Ramirez then asks everyone to say the word again, and they all enthusiastically say, "*Clutching*"! She calls on a few more children, and they tend to give similar comments about clutching a stuffed animal when they sleep at night. Ms. Ramirez had pulled a stuffed animal out of the library corner before her read-aloud to have her children demonstrate what clutching might look like during this step in her vocabulary sequence. She takes this opportunity to have each child demonstrate clutching the stuffed animal and then pass it on to the next child. As each child clutches the teddy bear, she asks them to tell her what they are doing and each child in turn says the word *clutching*. After each child has had a turn clutching the stuffed animal, Ms. Ramirez ends the discussion by having everyone repeat the word one final time. She says, "*What word did we talk about today that means to hold tightly?*" Each child responds with a resounding, "*Clutching*"! Ms. Ramirez tells them that they will talk about the words again tomorrow when they read and review *Brave Irene* (Steig, 1986) again.

Reflecting on the Reading

Ms. Ramirez has a set planning time every day when her class is in specials (e.g., art class). She uses this time to plan future lessons, gather materials, review assessments, or to meet with her grade-level team for planning or data-team meetings. The day after she implemented her read-aloud she takes some time to sit down and reflect on the new vocabulary sequence she introduced into her read-aloud repertoire with the book *Brave Irene* (Steig, 1986). She goes back to the planning template but this time completes the reflection and goal-setting columns. Ms. Ramirez makes it a regular practice to engage in self-reflection, but she likes this idea of completing a template that guides her through the entire teaching process. First, she completes the reflection column that asks her how she did by contrasting her original plans for vocabulary instruction and the actual lesson. She thinks carefully about how she weaved those strategies into her read-aloud and the resulting responses and interactions from her children. Last, she sets goals for improvement for her next read-aloud targeting vocabulary instruction. Ms. Ramirez's completed template is presented in Figure 4.7. Next, we take a look at Ms. Ramirez's reflective and goal-setting practices as she thinks about the strengths and the challenges of her read-aloud time.

Thinking about Strengths and Challenges

Ms. Ramirez feels a sense of accomplishment after her read-aloud time using *Brave Irene* (Steig, 1986). She also notes that there were a few future goals that she'd like to set. She moves through each strategy on the template in succession and reflects on that particular aspect of the read-aloud time and then sets a goal for the next reading. First, she reflects on *specific vocabulary word(s) introduced directly before and after reading*. She notes that she used the picture cards to introduce the words

A Focus on Vocabulary in Read-Alouds

	Planning What is my plan?	Reflecting How did I do?	Goal Setting What will I do next time?
Vocabulary Introduction (before and after reading)	brave and clutch brave: picture/word card with a firefighter going into burning building. clutch: picture/word card with a Mom holding her child's hand as they cross the street. Ask children to listen for the word in story (touch their ears).	I used the picture cards to introduce the words before and after reading. I think they helped the children to grasp the meaning of the words. They could easily identify with the words based on the pictures. It also helped me to explain the words.	I like the idea of creating picture cards for the wonderful words. I plan to add these to my vocabulary word wall/bulletin board for review. I will also try to make/find props for the words. This will help them to interact with the object to gain a real-world meaning of the words.
Vocabulary Infused into Storybook (during reading)	Pause when I come to the words in the story. Brave means to do something even if you might be scared and clutch means to hold onto to something very tightly. Check to see if children listened and touched their ears.	I paused when I came to these words and gave a brief, child-friendly definition. It was so wonderful to see most of my students touching their ears when I came to the word. They seem to love this strategy!	I plan to continue this strategy. I will plan for various types of every-pupil-response activities like giving a thumbs-up, tapping their head, touching their knees, etc. for variety and excitement.
Vocabulary Repeated (after reading)	After I introduce picture cards again and say the words, I will ask children to repeat the words brave and clutch.	I actually had my students say the words many, many times. I think this helps them to remember the words and they were enthusiastic about repeating the words.	The more the better! I will have them repeat the words several times. I hope that I hear them use the words beyond storybook time. I will plan to use the words in other contexts during the school day.
Vocabulary in Child-Friendly Terms (after reading)	After the children repeat the words, I will give them the child-friendly definitions of the words (same as the ones I gave during the reading).	I used the child-friendly definitions of the words right after students repeated the word. I also used my explanation of the picture cards to help explain the words. They quickly grasped the meaning of the words.	I will continue to plan child-friendly definitions. I noticed that I'm using Tier One words to define Tier Two words.
Vocabulary Contextualized (after reading)	Go back into the pages of the book and discuss how the words were used: Irene was brave when she took the dress to the duchess in the snowstorm and Irene clutched the box with the dress so she wouldn't drop it in the snow and the wind.	I went back into the book to explain how the words were used. I read the sentences with the words and then I gave it more of an explanation.	On the second reading, I will go back into the book and have them tell me how the words were used. I also plan to put tabs on the pages so that I can go quickly back into the book to find the pages.
Vocabulary in Other Contexts (after reading)	You are brave if you get a shot at the doctor's even though it might hurt or you're brave when you first learn how to ride a bike without training wheels. You might clutch your parent's hand when you cross the street or you might clutch your teddy bear when you sleep at night.	I provided two examples of each word outside of how the word was used in the story. I'm glad that I planned these ahead of time. The students liked my examples and it started them in thinking about how the word applies to them in their lives.	I will read the story again and have two additional uses of each word outside the story. I want them to see these words in as many contexts as possible so that they can apply the words in many ways.
Vocabulary Extended (after reading)	Ask children to give examples of the words: Is there a time when you had to be brave? Have you ever clutched anything? Can you show me how to clutch this baseball bat?	Students gave similar examples. I also used a prop for the word clutching to help them get an understanding of the word and an application of the word.	I think my students need additional exposures to the words. I will read the story again and offer more examples that may support them in their attempts to provide more types of examples of the words.

FIGURE 4.7. Ms. Ramirez's completed template.

before and after reading and that the cards assisted in helping the children to grasp the meaning of the words. She found that they easily identified with the words based on the pictures, and that they also provided her a pictorial example of the word in a real-world function. Her future goals include adding the picture cards to a vocabulary word wall in her classroom for review. She notes that she also wants to create or locate props for the words so that her children can interact with the props to gain a real-world meaning of the word.

She notes that for the next strategy, *specific word infused into the storybook*, she paused when she came to these words and gave a brief, child-friendly definition and that she was pleasantly surprised to see most of her children touching their ears when she came to the words. She notes that she will plan for various types of every-pupil-response activities like giving a thumbs-up, tapping their head, touching their knees, and so forth, for variety and excitement in future read-alouds targeting vocabulary development. For the next strategy, *specific words repeated*, Ms. Ramirez notes that she had her children repeat the words several times during the after-reading sequence. She thought that this helped the children to remember the words and they seemed to be enthusiastic about repeating them. Her goal is to see and hear them use the word beyond the book, so she will plan to use the words in other contexts during the school day.

Ms. Ramirez found that the use of *specific words in child-friendly terms* helped her children to quickly grasp the meaning of the words. She plans to continue creating her own child-friendly definitions for all words that she decides to target in her read-alouds. She realizes that this simply requires her to use Tier One words for more sophisticated Tier Two words. She notes that she then went back into the book to provide *a contextualized meaning of the word* and then provided an elaborated explanation of the word as it applied to the story. After she provided a contextualized meaning of the words, she provided the children with two additional examples of the *specific words in other contexts*. She's glad that she planned these examples ahead of time. She found that her children seemed to easily grasp her examples, and it assisted them in thinking about how the words apply to them in their lives outside school. Her goals include providing repeated readings and creating additional uses of the words outside the story. She wants to support her children by providing as many contexts as possible so that these words become part of their own vocabularies.

Finally, Ms. Ramirez reflects on the final strategy, *specific word examples from students*. She found that her children had difficulty in providing examples beyond the concept of clutching a stuffed animal. This may be because she provided each child a stuffed animal to demonstrate their understanding of *clutching*, and one of her examples outside of the story was of her brother clutching his teddy bear. She realizes that her children need additional exposures of the word. She will accomplish this by providing repeated readings of *Brave Irene* (Steig, 1986) with additional examples that may support them in their attempts to provide more types of examples of the word. She also plans to make these words a part of her home–school connection. She sends home a weekly newsletter to connect parents to the news and events of the classroom. She will add a section in her newsletter called, "Wonderful Words!" where she will highlight the wonderful words that her children are learning and encourage parents to use these same words with their children at home. Ms. Ramirez wants these words to live in her children's vocabularies forever.

Final Thoughts

Wonderful words come alive when you target vocabulary in your read-aloud time. A read-aloud time that infuses vocabulary strategies contains rich and robust discussion surrounding one or two specific words found in the story before, during, and after the reading. Read-aloud selections that are ideal for this strategy contain those wonderful words, captivating illustrations, interesting characters, and original story lines. We provided a useful, research-based vocabulary sequence of instruction to guide you in developing your children's vocabulary knowledge that includes (1) introducing the specific words before the reading, (2) providing child-friendly definitions of the words during the read-aloud, (3) reintroducing the words after the reading, (4) asking children to repeat the words, (5) giving a child-friendly definition of the words, (6) providing the use of the words in context, (7) listing several uses of the words outside of the story, and (8) encouraging children to provide uses of the words in their lives. We also provided a template (Figure 4.6) to assist you in planning these experiences in your read-aloud as well as the opportunity to reflect and set goals for future read-alouds. A blank planning template is presented in the Appendix for you to use to plan, reflect, and set goals for targeting vocabulary development in your future read-alouds.

CHAPTER 5

Developing Book and Print Conventions through Read-Alouds

Let's focus on the forms and functions of books and print! Book and print conventions refer to skills and abilities that you as an automatic and strategic reader have already developed. Print awareness is the ability to recognize the meaning of headings, the direction of reading, the position of books for reading, and other components that literate readers have but beginning readers need to develop. Someone who knows the conventions of print can determine how to hold a book, read its title, and read it by opening the front cover. A print-conventions competent reader also knows when beginning his or her reading to place his or her eyes and attention on the left side of a line, and while reading to move from the left of a line to its right, and from the top of a page to its bottom. Also, he or she knows when reaching the end of a line to return to the left of the following line and proceed with his or her reading. Print conventions vary depending on language; the conventions described in this chapter are ones common to English. It is important to be aware of differences in directionality across different linguistic cultures as they may have a different understanding on the regulations of print and its conventions.

Matching a Book to the Skill

Even students who cannot yet read words can and should learn the principles of reading. This knowledge will become a first step in their relationship with the printed world, hopefully a relationship that is long lasting and joyful. Selecting a book prior to your instruction is essential. Initially, it may appear easy to find a book for teaching print conventions because all books have letters and words. However, we have found that some books lend themselves to print-conventions instruction better than others. For example, print can be manipulated at the hands of a typographer to make a trace around a page, forcing the reader to read from corner to corner, or in a whirlpool manner (e.g., look at Figure 5.1). Even if these stylistic differences can astonish a strategic reader and cause his or her admiration for the author's creativity, they do not support a beginning reader who still struggles to differentiate between a picture and a word or between a word and a letter. Therefore, when selecting books for the instruction of this skill look for books that have a traditional orientation, presenting the letters, words, and lines in a left-to-right and top-to-bottom progression.

Besides orientation of text, you should be careful in the selection of text in which the letters are made of strokes and lines. Select books where the letters are large and have the traditional and conventional form that students will be taught while learning the alphabet. When drawing students' attention to letters in print, make sure the letters are clear and do not cause confusion.

An important component of book conventions is teaching students about the roles of authors and illustrators. When selecting books for instruction, look for sets of books in which the author and the illustrator are two different people and sets of books in which the author and illustrator are the same person. For example, Tomie dePaola is the author and the illustrator of most of his books. What a wonderful opportunity to teach your students that the same person can be the writer of the plot and also the creator of all the remarkable pictures. Distinguishing between the roles of author and illustrator cannot only help students with reading, but it can also motivate them to write and illustrate their own work.

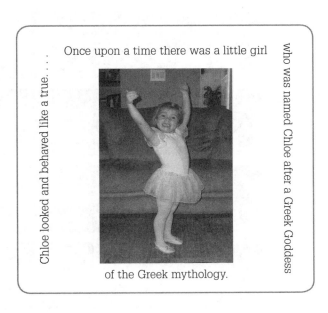

FIGURE 5.1. Stylistic differences in orientation of text.

Also, as you begin to make selections of books to use during print conventions instruction, try to locate books that have a variety of information provided on the front and back covers. In some books, the back cover provides a continuum of artwork introduced on the front cover. In other occasions, the back cover contains a list of other books written by the same author or at times commentary by critics. It is essential in your instruction to make the distinction between the content and function of the front cover and the back cover of a book. It is equally essential when your students are reading or pretend to read a book to identify the front and back covers.

Finally, as with choosing books for any type of instruction, it is important to consider student engagement. You should always look for books that can intrigue your students and attract their interest. Think about your own reading. Are you more likely to remember what you read if you can relate to the content in some way? The same is true for beginning readers. Therefore, select books that have interesting plots and themes. In Figure 5.2 we have a list of components you should look for when identifying books to teach print conventions.

We do not encourage you to purchase resources on new books, but to review your existing books with a critical eye. Revisit your children's literature collection to see which books you currently own that contain some or all of the characteristics described above and are ideal for supporting students' understanding of print and book conventions. In Figure 5.3, we have included a list of useful texts for teaching the concepts of print and book conventions.

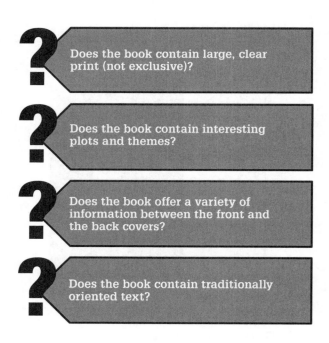

FIGURE 5.2. Components of books that support print conventions.

Fiction Selections	Nonfiction Selections
Little Toot by Hardie Gramatky (1997)	*The Tiny Seed* by Eric Carle (1987)
Corduroy by Dan Freeman (1968)	*How Do You Sleep?* by Louise Bonnett-Rampersaud (2005)
Caps for Sale by Esphyr Slobodkina (1947)	*A Bear Cub Grows Up* by Pam Zollman (2005a)
If You Give a Pig a Pancake by Laura Numeroff (1998)	*A Tadpole Grows Up* by Pam Zollman (2005c)
Guess How Much I Love You by Sam McBratey (1995)	*A Turtle Hatching Grows Up* by Pam Zollman (2005d)
The Snowy Day by Ezra Jack Keats (1962)	*A Spiderling Grows Up* by Pam Zollman (2005b)

FIGURE 5.3. Books on our shelves to develop print conventions.

Deciding How to Develop the Skill

Under the umbrella of print conventions are specific subskills. Research findings indicate that these subskills, when embedded in instruction, support students in developing a clear understanding of the functions of print. In this section we discuss each subskill and the guidelines for introducing and reviewing them with young students during read-alouds.

The front and back of the book are two subcomponents of print conventions (Clay, 1991). A reader needs to be able to identify the front and back of the book and the information each provides (Lovelace & Stewart, 2007). In initial instruction you can point to the front of the book and explain what the purpose of an inviting front cover is. You can explicitly show the front cover, say what it is, and then ask your students to repeat the information. Gradually, you will be able to invite your students to point to and identify the front cover or back cover of a book. It is important not only to have your students identify the covers by pointing but also by naming. As students become more familiar with identifying the front of a book, you will be able to expand your instruction to elaborate on the purpose of a front cover. Usually the artwork on the cover provides a glimpse of what the book will be about. Also, its inviting artwork can potentially attract the interest of the reader to select it.

In addition, you can discuss and explain the role of the author and the role of the illustrator/photographer. It is essential for students to be able to identify the writer of the words of a book and differentiate this role from the role of the illustrator or photographer and vice versa (Justice & Ezell, 2000, 2002, 2004; Justice et al., 2002). Students need to know that the author is the writer and the one who develops the ideas and plot of the book. In your instruction you should name the author and state his or her role. You can follow the same procedure when introducing the illustrator or photographer and explain that he or she is responsible for the artwork or photographs. You may also want to discuss the relationship between the author and illustrator in creating the book. Conventionally in children's books the pictures elaborate or support the meaning of the words. Both the author and the illustrator are individually creative, but also collaborate to create a coherent message. In some cases the same person is both the author and the illustrator. Nevertheless, the students need to be able to identify what the person did as an author and as an illustrator.

Knowing where to look for the title of the book and for the title page is also a subskill of print conventions essential for a beginning reader. Readers know that the titles of books contain information and clues about the content of the book (Clay, 1991; Justice & Ezell, 2000, 2002, 2004; Justice et al., 2002, 2006; Lovelace & Stewart, 2007). Therefore, they need to be able to locate the title. To support your students you can point to the title of a book and say, "This is the title of the book. It says _____. What does it say?" When pointing to and explaining the title of the book, you may discuss with your students the differences in the font the title is written in or the location of the title on the cover or on the page. A book title will be at the top of the book or at its center in large letters. When looking at the title page with students, you can consider what the page is called and what appears on the page. For example, during reading, you may call students' attention to the title page: "This is the title page. What is it? On the title page I see. . . . "

Book and print conventions in English are different from conventions in other languages, such as Arabic. This difference is based not only on the letter formation and use of symbols, but also on directionality of print and conventions of reading. These are specific aspects of language that students need to know early on so they will know where and how to look at a text (Lovelace & Stewart, 2007; NELP, 2007; van Kleek, 1995). When introducing the top-to-bottom progression you need to be direct in your explanation. For example, when looking at a page of a book with students you would say, "There are seven lines on this page. I will read from this line [point to the first line] and then move to the next one and the next one until I reach the last line. When I read, I will move from the top of the page to the bottom of the page. You will see my pointing finger move from line to line. When you read on your own, you will read from line to line from top to bottom."

Left-to-right progression is one of the characteristics of English that students also need to know. In your instruction you will model and track the print following this direction so your students will internalize the progression of printed words. In your instruction point to the left of the line and say, "When I read I start from here and then move to this side." When you point make sure to show the movement of your finger through the tracking of words. You do not want to give the impression that you leaped from the first mark of the line to the last one of the same line. When you are practicing with your students you may call them to point as you read using their "reading finger" or a pointer you may have in class. A pointer can be very helpful in allowing all students to have a common view when you are reading to your whole class. And students will delight in using your pointer when called on to identify an important print or book convention. Sometimes, however, pointers can be heavy for young students to manipulate and as a result may affect their ability to physically track print on a page.

Return sweep is a challenging aspect of our language. When a young child first approaches text on a page, he or she may be tempted to read the first line of a text, come to the end, move to the word directly underneath the last word of the first line, and continue to read the second line from right to left. Knowing though that our language has a left-to-right progression, it would make sense to return to the left side every time. For young readers the challenge may be identifying the line they should look to when returning to the left. Have you ever worked with a child who skipped a line at the return sweep? It is pretty typical for young children to lose track of which line to return to while reading or following print. This act requires knowledge of the print convention as well as coordination of eye and finger movement. In your modeling you can explicitly show how you return back to the first word of the next line, and in follow-up sessions you can ask your students to guide you in what direction you go next to read.

Counting words in a sentence and counting letters in words are two additional subskills that should not be undervalued either (Justice & Ezell, 2000, 2002, 2004; Justice et al., 2002; Morris et al., 2003). Children hear the stream of words in a continuum and find it difficult to try and differentiate where one word ends and the next begins in oral speech. When working in print, though, you can model for them that a sentence contains a number of words that when read together have a complete meaning for the reader. This breaking down of words within a sentence supports students' understanding of language use and print structure. Finally, counting letters within a word supports the students' understanding that not all words have the same length and that their length is determined by the number of letters and not other factors that may derive from the referring action or object.

All of the procedures for print and book conventions require that you model and review the names of the subskills and their application with students over multiple read-alouds. It is essential to be as explicit as possible so your students will know how to process text and why. In Figure 5.4 we have included the list of best practices for the development of print conventions. We hope you will find it helpful when you are preparing your read-alouds and want to confirm research-based instructional practices. Remember that in the process of your introduction and constant modeling you can be as creative as possible and make this procedure fun.

Planning Template

Next, we will follow Mrs. Tragas, a kindergarten teacher, as she uses a planning template to focus on teaching book and print conventions during read-alouds. Mrs. Tragas is a second-year teacher and works at Kalowell Elementary school in the suburbs of a major metropolitan area. Her class consists of 14 boys and 12 girls. Out of her 26 students, 11 have attended preschool. Also, 5 of her students are second-language learners and have not attended preschool. Finally, three of her students are registered with Child Study and their academic progress is monitored.

Near the beginning of the school year, Mrs. Tragas realizes that many of her young students have had limited exposure to print and book conventions, especially the students who did not attend preschool. Mrs. Tragas decides that she needs to

Front of Book	Model and/or invite students to identify front of book and encourage entire group to name the part of the book.
Back of Book	Model and/or invite students to identify back of book and encourage entire group to name the part of the book.
Title of Book	Model and/or invite students to point to the title of book.
Title Page	Model and/or invite students to point to or name the title page.
Role of the Author	Model and/or invite students to discuss the role of the author.
Role of the Illustrator/ Photographer	Model and/or invite students to discuss the role of the illustrator.
Top-to-Bottom Progression	Model and/or invite students to demonstrate top-to-bottom progression.
Left-to-Right Progression	Model and/or invite students to demonstrate left-to-right progression.
Return Sweep	Model and/or invite students to demonstrate return sweep by moving finger from end of line back to the left on the next line of text.
Count Words	Model and/or invite students to count words on a title or page/sentence.
Count Letters in a Word	Model and/or invite students to count letters in a word.

FIGURE 5.4. Best practices in the development of print conventions.

model print and book conventions in repeated read-alouds throughout the year to build her students' background knowledge with the conventions. For one of her read-alouds, Mrs. Tragas chooses to read the book *Little Toot* by Hardie Gramatky (2002). She has a big version of the book (big book), and she thinks that the big version will allow all of her students to see her providing instruction on book and print conventions. Prior to reading the book, Mrs. Tragas planned her lesson using the planning template. You will find the completed planning section of the template in Figure 5.5. A blank version of the template is available in the Appendix (Form 3). After completing the planning section, Mrs. Tragas asked her students to gather at the circle in their designated carpet spots. We will follow her as she conducts her read-aloud.

Implementing the Reading

Mrs. Tragas was aware of her students' needs regarding the development of print awareness and book conventions. Prior to selecting a book for her read-aloud, she thoughtfully planned the focus of her lesson and the ways she could involve her students. For this read-aloud, she decided to use a big book, as its content would be more visible to her students. Also, it would allow students to point to the lines when she asked them to repeat her actions, and she would be able to better monitor what they did and how. In the book Mrs. Tragas selected, the print was such that it allowed her to point out how a sentence could start and finish on one line and how

A Focus on Book and Print Conventions in Read-Alouds

	Planning What is my plan?	Reflecting How did I do?	Goal Setting What will I do next time?
Front of Book	I will ask the students to identify the front of the book.		
Back of Book	I will ask the students to show the back cover of the book.		
Title of Book	I will point to the title and read it and ask a student or more than one student to repeat.		
Title Page	NA		
Role of Author	I will read the name of the author and ask the students to explain his or her role.		
Role of Illustrator and Photographer	I will read the name of the illustrator/photographer and ask the students to explain his or her role.		
Top-to-Bottom Progression	I will point to the number of lines and show the top to bottom direction for reading.		
Left-to-Right Progression	I will track the print and ask a student to track the print.		
Return Sweep	I will model return sweep and ask students to direct me to the next line as I read.		
Count Words	I will model and ask the students to count the words on the title page and count the words in the sentences of selected pages.		
Count Letters in a Word	I will ask the students to count the letters in the words *little* and *toot* in the title.		

FIGURE 5.5. Mrs. Tragas's initial planning template.

it could continue to different lines. The content of the book was also engaging, and there was a balance between written text and pictures.

Mrs. Tragas asked her students to gather around the circle and prepared for the reading of the book. In the next section, you will read a snapshot of her lesson.

Teacher Talk during Read-Alouds

One morning Mrs. Tragas gathers her students on the carpet and says, "*Good morning. Today we are going to read a new book. As we read we are going to pay attention to print conventions. Remember that good readers know where to look when they read and how to move their eyes and reading finger on a page. We are going to continue learning and practicing all our skills today. So, let me ask you, where is the front cover of this book? Lianna, would you like to show us?*"

Lianna sits up and points to the front cover, saying, "*This is the front cover.*" Then Lianna turns the book and says, "*And this is the back cover of the book.*"

Mrs. Tragas congratulates her student and says, "*That is correct, Lianna. This is the front cover and this is the back cover.*" Mrs. Tragas turns the book for the class to see. "*Remember what we have said about the front cover of a book? It can give us valuable information. It can tell us the title of the book, the author, the illustrator, and through wonderful pictures it can help us understand what the book will be about. So, the title of the book is **Little Toot**.*" As Mrs. Tragas reads the title, she sweeps her finger under it. "*Who can read the title for me? Mario, would you like to read the title?*"

Mario approaches and with his finger points to each word as he reads the title.

"*That is excellent, Mario! I will now count the words in my title. Watch me as I count the words. The title is **Little Toot**. In the title I have one, two words. Who would like to count the title words?*" Mrs. Tragas looked at her students who had raised their hands patiently waiting for her to select someone to respond to her question. "*Zayra, would you like to count the words?*"

Zayra approaches Mrs. Tragas and, using her finger, she begins counting the words: "*One, two for **Little Toot!***"

"*Excellent, Zayra!*" says Mrs. Tragas. "*Now watch me as I count the letters within the first word of the title, the word **little**. I will use my pointing finger. Watch me: one, two, three, four, five, six letters. Who would like to count the letters for the word **little**?*" Mrs. Tragas looks at her students and then calls on Nicholas.

Nicholas approaches and Mrs. Tragas first asks him to point to the word and count the letters of the word *little*. Nicholas counts, "*One, two, three, four, five.*" What Nicholas does is to skip the second *t* in the word, and count it only once. Mrs. Tragas says, "*That was such a nice effort, Nicholas. Watch me as I count the letters one more time.*" Mrs. Tragas counts the letters and explains that even if the letter *t* repeats in the word, it has to be counted again as this is how the word is spelled/written. Nicholas repeats after her and does the task correctly.

Mrs. Tragas repeats the same procedure with the word *toot* and Nicholas completes the task correctly.

Mrs. Tragas continues, "*The author of the book has a long name. He is Hardie Gramatky. Who is the author? Use your lion voices to tell me the author.*" The students with roaring voices repeat the author's name. Mrs. Tragas says, "*I wonder what an author does and why his or her name should be on the book? George, would you like to remind us of the role of the author?*"

George, from his seat, says, "*He writes the words.*"

Mrs. Tragas agrees, "*Yes, the author is the one who writes all the wonderful words we read in a story. When you write your stories, you are authors in the same way. Books, though, have someone else who is mentioned on the front cover. Who is that, Marcell?*"

Marcell replies, "*The illustrator and he make the pictures.*"

"*That is correct, Marcell!*" says Mrs. Tragas with a smile. "*In this book, though, I cannot see the name of the illustrator. Sometimes books have only one name; when this happens the author and the illustrator is the same person. In this book, the name of the illustrator is on the first page of the book. The illustrator is Mark Burgess. Who is the illustrator? Use your ant voices to tell me.*"

Mrs. Tragas reads the name of the illustrator, and the students repeat his name with low-decibel voices.

"*Excellent!*" praises Mrs. Tragas. "*We will now look at the first page of the book. How many lines of text do I have here? Who can count for me and point to the lines? Zola, would you like to do that?*"

Zola approaches the book and counts without pointing. There are a total of four lines, but Zola says there are six. Mrs. Tragas reminds Zola to use his counting finger, point, and count. Zola counts again and says, "*There are five lines.*"

Mrs. Tragas gently corrects, "*There are four lines, Zola. Look: one, two, three, four.*" Then she continues, "*So when I read I move from this line,*" pointing to the first line, "*to this line, then this one, and end at the last line,*" pointing to the second, third, and fourth lines. "*Could you show us, Zola, what line I begin reading?*" Zola points to the first line.

"*Great job, Zola! So I will begin reading the first line. When I read I always begin reading from here, and I move to this side,*" says Mrs. Tragas as she uses her finger to point from one word to the next from left to right. "*Gavin, could you show us where I will start reading and the direction I will read?*"

Gavin approaches the big book and points to the first word, moving his finger across the line and then pointing to the end of the line.

"*That was great, Gavin!*" said Mrs. Tragas. "*How will I read line two? Peter, would you like to show us?*"

Peter approaches the book and moves his finger across the line. Mrs. Tragas continues this practice with all the lines on the page. Then she tells her students, "*It can be tricky when I read and I reach the end of the line. When I am at the end of the line I need to return to the beginning of the next line. This can be challenging, but I need to pay attention and move my reading finger from the end of the one line to the start of the next line. So when I read I will move my finger like this.*" Mrs. Tragas moves her finger across the first line, returns to the beginning of the second line, moves it across the second line, returns to the beginning of the third line, and does the same for the last line of text. Then she asks, "*Who would like to show us how we are to read when reading the four lines? Katie? Would you like to show our class?*"

Katie uses her reading finger to repeat the process that her teacher demonstrated. Mrs. Tragas encourages Katie and then continues the read-aloud. "*Now I will begin my reading. I will put my reading finger at the start of the first line, move it across, and then return to the next line.*" Mrs. Tragas begins reading the book. She follows the procedure of pointing and reading for the entire book.

At the end of the book Mrs. Tragas says, "*I have reached the end of the book, and I will close the book so we can see the back cover of the book. That was nice reading we did. Remember that when we read, we use our reading finger and read from the top of the page and from one side—our left side—to the other side—our right side. We will practice more while reading other books.*"

Reflecting on the Reading

After completing the reading, Mrs. Tragas reviewed her planning goals and then recalled the lesson. In general, she was satisfied with the students' performance. The students were able to provide correct answers.

Something that worried her, though, was that, fearing time would run short, she had the tendency to call only on one student to repeat her modeled action. She realized that asking only one student did not give other students an opportunity for practice. Also, she realized that she did not ask the students to count words within a sentence across the reading because she feared extending the reading time. Therefore, she sets the goal to include more than one student in her future read-alouds. She even considered dividing a book into several read-alouds instead of trying to complete the whole reading in one session. Mrs. Tragas set asking more than one student across all skills a general goal and recorded that across the "Goal Setting" column of her template. In addition, she noticed that Nicholas, when asked to count the letters within the word *little*, counted the letter *t* only once. Mrs. Tragas interpreted this mistake as confusion due to the repetition of the letter and the student's tendency to count uniquely appearing letters in a sequence. However, she now realized that this was her own interpretation, and she still did not know what her student thought. Nevertheless, she was glad to see that Nicholas was able, after her modeling, to repeat the task correctly and also count the letters correctly in the word *toot*, which also repeated the letter *o*. Mrs. Tragas also noted that Lianna showed both the front and the back cover of the book. The latter was something that another student could have done in class, or she could have asked someone else to repeat after Lianna in order to increase student participation.

Also, Mrs. Tragas remembered that the book she selected had the name of the author on the front cover, but the name of the illustrator on the inside page. This could have been confusing to some of her students. The general information she had given them about the location of the author and illustrator was incorrect. In order to avoid any misunderstandings, Mrs. Tragas set as her goal reading a different book that had the name of the author and illustrator on the front cover next time.

Mrs. Tragas also recalled that she was not as consistent in tracking print. For example, she just read the name of the illustrator, but did not point to the words, which could have explained why her students were not consistent in pointing to the words as well. Her new goal is to consistently track print while reading aloud. Also, she thought of Zola, who had trouble counting by tracking. Perhaps his difficulty was due to her poor modeling. Mrs. Tragas also thought that in cases of a mistake she should set as her goal repeating the modeling with the student and allowing him or her to repeat on his or her own. For example, with Zola she could have guided his finger while counting and then asked him to count after her.

Finally, Mrs. Tragas realized that even if she was very explicit at the introductory section of her lesson, she rushed through the reading without stopping and asking students to show her how they moved from line to line, or asking students to point to the text as she read. Mrs. Tragas set as her goal including student practice throughout the book instead of limiting their participation due to time constraints. In Figure 5.6 you can see the completed template based on Mrs. Tragas's reflections.

Final Thoughts

Print and book conventions support the development of a first understanding on how written language functions. Your students will learn from direct instruction of the conventions during read-alouds and may even begin to experiment on their own, performing "pretend readings" of texts where they point to the title, author, or even the lines of text as they read. We hope that the suggestions we provided will assist you in selecting texts and planning your read-aloud to develop students' print and book conventions. We also expect that the blank planning template will support you in the process of evaluating and reflecting on your instruction and students' learning. We wish you nothing less than happy tracking of print.

A Focus on Book and Print Conventions in Read-Alouds

	Planning What is my plan?	Reflecting How did I do?	Goal Setting What will I do next time?
Front of Book	I will ask the students to identify the front of the book.	I did ask Lianna to show the front cover and she did well.	Ask more than one student.
Back of Book	I will ask the students to show the back cover of the book.	Lianna also showed the back cover of the book.	I should ask different students so everyone will have an opportunity to participate.
Title of Book	I will point to the title and read it and ask a student or more than one student to repeat.	The students were able to repeat the title and point to the title of the book. However, Mario didn't really read by pointing. He just read the title fast without really tracking the print.	Ask more than one student. Model how to point underneath the title when reading it. Read the title slowly as the students may try to repeat reading fast as I did.
Title Page	NA		
Role of Author	I will read the name of the author and ask the students to explain his or her role.	George did a good job explaining the role of the author.	Ask more than one student.
Role of Illustrator and Photographer	I will read the name of the illustrator/photographer and ask the students to explain his or her role.	It may have been confusing that the illustrator was not on the front cover. The students did not show signs of confusion, but I should be more explicit next time. I did not point to the name of the author when I read it.	Ask more than one student. Use a book that lists both author and illustrator at the front cover. Always track the print when reading.
Top-to-Bottom Progression	I will point to the number of lines and show the top-to-bottom direction for reading.	I called on Zola to count the lines. I could have counted with him by guiding his finger instead of doing it on my own. Then he could have repeated it. After, I could have stressed the importance of top-to-bottom for reading.	Ask more than one student. Correct the students and model with them, model myself (if needed), and allow them to repeat on their own and give feedback.
Left-to-Right Progression	I will track the print and ask a student to track the print.	Peter did a good job tracking. But I didn't ask other students to try.	Ask more than one student.

(continued)

FIGURE 5.6. Mrs. Tragas's completed template.

	Planning What is my plan?	Reflecting How did I do?	Goal Setting What will I do next time?
Return Sweep	I will model return sweep and ask students to direct me to the next line as I read.	I did not ask the students to tell me where I should move when I was reading the text.	Ask more than one student. Ask for the students to show their understanding not only at the introduction of the lesson, but throughout the reading.
Count Words	I will model and ask the students to count the words on the title page and count the words in the sentences of selected pages.	I did ask the students to count the words on the title page, but due to time I did not ask them to repeat the procedure in sentences.	I need to make sure that the students count words in a sentence and get accustomed to sentence boundaries throughout the book. I should split the reading into sections.
Count Letters in a Word	I will ask the students to count the letters in the words *little* and *toot* in the title.	Nicholas seemed to struggle with the repeating letter of the word. I should have asked to understand the reason for his confusion.	Ask more than one student. I should repeat the process with other students and perhaps identify the reason for their confusion when encountering repeated letters in a sequence.

FIGURE 5.6. *(continued)*

CHAPTER 6

Developing Alphabet Awareness through Read-Alouds

Read-alouds develop children's alphabet knowledge! When teachers name or ask children to name letters during reading, they are building letter identification skills. When teachers call attention to the sounds letters make, they are building letter–sound correspondence. Letter identification and letter–sound correspondence are essential skills for children to develop the alphabetic principle. The alphabetic principle is the knowledge that individual letters make individual sounds (Adams, 1990) and is an important foundational step toward future reading (Adams, 1990; IRA/NAEYC, 1998). Children ultimately use their knowledge of letter sounds to help them sound out words while reading. As a teacher of young children you have an important role to play in fostering children's emerging alphabet awareness.

Planning the Reading

Planning to target alphabet awareness during read-alouds involves careful consideration of the skill, the text, and the instructional activity. The first step should be to decide on which alphabet skill or skills to develop. The skills associated with alphabet awareness include (1) letter identification and (2) letter-sound knowledge. Letter identification is the ability to identify a letter's name. A child pointing to the letter *T* and saying "Tee" is demonstrating his or her skill at letter identification. Letter-sound knowledge is the ability to produce the sound an individual letter or letter combination makes. For example, when a teacher asks what sound the letter *B* makes, a child responding /b/ has letter-sound knowledge. You may choose to target one skill or a combination of the skills in a single read-aloud depending on the skill level of the children in your classroom and your goal for instruction at that time.

Once a skill is chosen, however, the next step in planning involves selecting a good book.

Matching a Book to a Skill

In a sense, any written text provides an opportunity for targeting children's alphabet awareness. You can call attention to letters of the alphabet in any text you are reading with children. However, some texts are especially well suited for alphabet instruction either through format or content.

Format is particularly important when focusing on letter identification skills with children. Some texts have a format that highlights the shape of letters on the page as a text feature, setting individual letters apart through a change in color, size, font, or spacing. This special text feature helps when calling attention to individual letters while reading a book with multiple children, often making it easier for children to see the letters on the page. Similarly, texts with large print, such as texts printed in big book format, are conducive for alphabet study with children.

Other texts lend themselves to work on alphabet awareness because of their content. A specific category of picture books referred to as alphabet books focus on the letters of the alphabet as their subject (Johnson, 2009). Many alphabet books present an illustration of something that begins with each letter of the alphabet, proceeding through the alphabet with one letter per page. For example, the first page of a text might feature a picture of an alligator and the letter *A* in upper case and lower case so that children can begin to associate an object with its beginning letter. Other alphabet books create memorable stories about the letters to help teach alphabetic order and the names of the letters. Examples of alphabet books structured around a story include the rhythmic *Chicka Chicka Boom Boom* (Martin & Archambault, 2009) and the series *Alphabet Adventure, Alphabet Mystery*, and *Alphabet Rescue* (Wood, 2001, 2003, 2006, respectively). Some alphabet books use the letters of the alphabet as an organizational structure to teach content (Johnson, 2009). For example, the book *H is for Home Run: A Baseball Alphabet* (Herzog, 2004) uses the alphabet as a way to organize content about the game of baseball, including its history, famous players, and rules of the game. An additional set of alphabet books are interactive, challenging children to find the letters hidden in pictures. For example, *Alphabet City* (Johnson, 1999) is a collection of photographs from city scenes in which everyday objects resemble letters of the alphabet.

The good news is that there are numerous alphabet books available for use with young children. In fact, there are so many that it is almost impossible to think of a topic that does not have an alphabet book associated with it. This makes it relatively easy for you to find an alphabet book to match your current unit or themes addressed in your curriculum. For example, if you work on a thematic unit involving dinosaurs, you can easily find several alphabet books incorporating dinosaur names in their presentation of the alphabet. Similarly, you can also find alphabet books to match individual children's interests. For example, within your classroom library collection you can include alphabet books for the child who loves superheroes, the child who loves flowers, the child who loves sports, and so on. Figure 6.1 presents a list of some of our favorite alphabet books to use with young children.

The downside to having so many alphabet books available is that choosing which ones to use in your classroom can be overwhelming. We recommend keeping three things in mind when selecting them for use with young children: audience, purpose, and quality. In terms of audience, consider your children's reading levels and interests. Purpose includes instruction of both specific alphabet skills, including letter identification, letter–sound correspondence, letter formation, and more general content connections with the thematic unit under study. Determining the quality of alphabet books can involve multiple criteria, including your own judgments

---

A to Z by Sandra Boynton (1984)

Eric Carle's ABC by Eric Carle (2007)

A Is for Artist by Ella Doran (2005)

The Alphabet Book by P. D. Eastman (1974)

Q Is for Duck: An Alphabet Guessing Game by Mary Elting and Michael Folsom (2005)

The Turn-Around, Upside-Down Alphabet Book by Lisa Campbell Ernest (2004)

The Dangerous Alphabet by Neil Gaiman (2008)

The Absolutely Awful Alphabet by Mordicai Gerstein (2001

H Is for Home Run: A Baseball Alphabet by Brad Herzog (2004)

ABC: A Child's First Alphabet Book by Alison Jay (2003)

Alphabet City by Stephen T. Johnson (1999)

AlphaOops! The Day Z Went First by Althea Kontis (2006)

On Market Street by Arnold Lobel (1981)

Chicka Chicka Boom Boom: Anniversary Edition by Bill Martin Jr. and John Archambault (2009)

SuperHero ABC by Bob McLeod (2008)

The Underwater Alphabet Book by Jerry Pallotta (1991)

The Graphic Alphabet by David Pelletier (1996)

Into the A, B, Sea: An Ocean Alphabet Book by Deborah Lee Rose (2001)

The Butterfly Alphabet by Kjell Bloch Sandved (1999)

Dr. Seuss's ABC: An Amazing Alphabet Book! by Dr. Seuss

Tomorrow's Alphabet by George Shannon (1999)

An A to Z Walk in the Park by R. M. Smith (2008)

Shiver Me Letters: A Pirate ABC by June Sobel (2009)

The Z Was Zapped: A Play in Twenty-Six Acts by Chris Van Allsburg (1987)

Alphabet Adventure by Audrey Wood (2001)

Alphabet Mystery by Audrey Wood (2003)

Alphabet Rescue by Audrey Wood (2006)

FIGURE 6.1. Alphabet books on our shelves.

about the book format, illustrations, text, and content. Figure 6.2 summarizes the criteria for choosing alphabet books.

Deciding How to Develop the Skill

Once you have chosen a text to use for alphabet instruction, you must determine how to develop alphabet awareness skills within the book context. Research has identified four best practices that can be embedded during reading to effectively teach alphabet knowledge to young children: (1) identifying any letter, (2) identifying a specific letter, (3) identifying a letter in a child's name, and (4) making the connection between a letter and its sound explicit. Figure 6.3 summarizes best practices in developing alphabet knowledge during read-alouds.

Perhaps the most basic technique you can use while reading is to identify any letter by its name (Adams, 1990; Cardoso-Martins, Resende, & Rodrigues, 2002; Justice et al., 2002; Morris et al., 2003). With young children just learning the letter names for the first time or with children who are struggling with alphabet knowledge, you can model naming letters on a page of the book. For example, you may point to the letter *K* and say, "I am going to name a letter on this page. This is the letter *K*. What letter?" As children become more familiar with letters, you can invite them to name any letter on a page. For example, you can elicit participation

Audience
• Who will be reading the text? • At what reading levels are the readers? • What subjects are of interest to the readers? • Is the alphabet presented in a manner that will be of interest to the children?
Purpose
• Will the text be useful for teaching letter identification? • Will the text be useful for teaching letter–sound correspondence? • Will the text be useful for teaching letter formation? • Does the text connect to the curriculum or thematic unit under study?
Quality
• Is the format of the text conducive to teaching young children the alphabet? • How is the text organized? From *A–Z*, *Z–A*, or some other system? • Do the illustrations support learning the names of letters, the sounds of letters, or how to form the letters? • Do the pictures related to each letter accurately portray the letter's sound? • Are the letters easy to see and recognize on the page? • Does the subject contribute to a unified, believable presentation of the alphabet? Or does the link between the subject and the alphabet seem contrived?

FIGURE 6.2. Criteria for selecting alphabet books.

Best Practice	Description
Identify any letter.	Model and/or invite students to name any letter on a page.
Identify specific letter/letters.	Models and/or invite students to name a specific letter/letters on a page.
Identify a letter in the student's own name.	Model and/or invite student to name a letter on a page that contains a letter in his or her own name.
Teach sound–symbol correspondence.	Make a direct connection to a letter and the sound by showing the letter, having the students name the letter and sound, and provide words that begin with that sound.

FIGURE 6.3. Summary of best practices for developing alphabet knowledge.

by choosing a child and asking him or her to come up to the book to point to and name a letter.

A related activity is to focus instruction on specific letters (Adams, 1990; Clay, 1991; Neuman et al., 2000). You may decide to model this activity first by pausing on a page and saying, "I am looking for the letter O on this page." You can then point to the letter O and say, "Here is the letter O. What letter is this?" You can also invite children to participate by calling up a child to the book and asking, "Can you point to the letter R on this page?" Once the child has located and pointed to an R, you can turn to either the individual child or the whole class and ask, "What letter did we find?"

Young children have a special affinity for the letters in their names. Have you ever met a child who has not fallen in love with the letters in his or her name? Capitalize on this connection by asking children to identify letters in their names (Adams, 1990; Justice & Ezell, 2002; NELP, 2007). For example, modeling identifying letters in a name, Mrs. Childs may point to the letter C and say, "I see the letter C on this page. I have the letter C in my name, too." Writing her name on the chalkboard, Mrs. Childs continues, "Here is the letter C on the page and here is the letter C in my name." Then she can invite children to participate by calling a child up to the book and asking, "Can you name a letter on this page that is also a letter in your name?"

All of the techniques described so far develop children's letter identification. You can also draw children's attention to the correspondence between letters and their sounds during reading (Adams, 1990; McFadden, 1998; NRP, 2000; Ukrainetz, Cooney, Dyer, Kysar, & Harris, 2000). For example, you can make a direct connection to a letter and the sound that it makes by showing the letter on the page, having the children name the letter and its sound, and providing example words that begin with that sound. You may pause on a page while reading to point to a letter and ask, "What letter is this?" When children respond, you can either model the sound the letter makes or ask, "What sound does it make?" When children respond, you can provide examples of words that begin with that same sound or ask, "Can you think of any words that begin with that sound?"

Planning Template

We have created the template presented in Figure 6.4 to help guide your thinking about alphabet instruction during read-alouds. The template lists the four best practices for alphabet instruction within read-alouds described above in the left-hand column and provides additional space for planning alphabet-infused read-alouds, reflecting on the success of alphabet instruction within read-alouds once it has been tried in the classroom, and setting goals for improving alphabet instruction in future read-alouds. A blank version of the template is available in the Appendix (Form 4).

To illustrate using the template, we describe Mrs. Greene, a kindergarten teacher working in a public elementary school. Mrs. Greene's class consists of 19 boys and girls from a range of socioeconomic backgrounds. A few of Mrs. Greene's students are learning English as a second language; in addition, a few students have individualized education plans (IEPs) for documented disabilities. The school in which Mrs. Greene works uses a half-day model, providing one kindergarten day in the morning and one in the afternoon. However, the school provides parents of children who are struggling the option of allowing their child to attend both sessions for an extended day of enrichment activities. Mrs. Greene spends a lot of her time on the letters of the alphabet over the course of the school year, weaving alphabet instruction into the morning routine with morning message and singing the alphabet song, literacy centers children participate in throughout the reading instructional block, and even within her comments to children during transitions, such as, "You are standing as straight as a letter *I* in line today." Despite her careful focus on alphabet instruction, Mrs. Greene feels that she can do even more. Specifically, she has targeted her read-aloud as a time to infuse more alphabet instruction during her day.

While planning for an upcoming unit on community, Mrs. Greene chooses the alphabet book *Alphabet Rescue* (Wood, 2006) for a read-aloud. Since the alphabet letters work together as a team to fight a fire in the story, the text connects well with the curricular community theme. In addition, as an alphabet book the text has several features that will enable alphabet instruction while students read. First, the story uses the letters of the alphabet as characters participating in the action, making a real focus on the letters themselves. The letters as the characters of the story are set within real contexts in the illustrations; for example, in one scene the letters of the alphabet are riding on a fire truck. Second, certain letters that play a central role in the action are highlighted in red, setting them apart in the written text. Finally, the illustrations present three-dimensional upper- and lower-case letters, each in a different color, making them stand out from one another.

Once Mrs. Greene has selected the text, she sits down to plan her read-aloud. Opening the book to the front-end page, Mrs. Greene notices right away a colorful, complete alphabet from *A* to *Z*. Since all of the letters are on the same page in upper case and lower case and organized alphabetically, the page makes a great place to pause and ask children to identify any letter they know. Since the letters are presented in alphabetical order, the students even have an aid for letter identification; if they need to, they can sing the letters as they point to them. Mrs. Greene makes

A Focus on Alphabet Awareness in Read-Alouds

	Planning What is my plan?	Reflecting How did I do?	Goal Setting What will I do next time?
Identify Any Letter	I will pause when opening the book to the front-end page and call on one or two children to identify any letters they know on the page. I will repeat this after reading on the back-end page if there is time.		
Identify Specific Letter/ Letters	Whenever I come to a page that has a letter highlighted in red, I will pause after reading and ask children to identify the specific letter highlighted.		
Identify a Letter in Child's Own Name	After every two or three pages, I will pause after reading and invite children to search the illustrations to find letters in their own names.		
Sound–Symbol Correspondence	I will model the sound the letter L makes on page 2, saying the letter name and sound and asking students to repeat with me. Throughout the text I will drag out the sound the letter L makes.		

FIGURE 6.4. Mrs. Greene's initial planning template.

a note to begin the reading by calling on a few children to identify any letters they know on the front-end page and then, if there is time, repeat the same activity on the back-end page of the book.

Next, Mrs. Greene likes that a few letters are highlighted in red within the written text. For example, when describing something said by Fire Chief F, the text highlights the letter *F* by printing it in red. Mrs. Greene thinks this text feature will lend itself to asking children to identify specific letters. She plans to read the text on a page and then pause to ask a child to come up to the book to point to a specific letter like the letter *F*. While reading she can point out that the letter *F* is in red, and then children can use the red letter as a support when asked to identify another letter *F* on the same page. Mrs. Greene records where letters are highlighted in red in the text and plans to pause on these pages to ask children to identify specific letters. She finds she can target letters *F*, *E*, *X*, *B*, *R*, *N*, and *C* using this activity.

A striking feature of the book is the colorful illustrations. Mrs. Greene anticipates that her students are going to be drawn to looking at the illustrations, which include all of the letters of the alphabet in different colors. Because the letters are spread out within each of the different scenes, Mrs. Greene decides to engage children in finding very important letters—the letters in their names—within the illustrations. She plans to pause after every two or three pages to provide children time to play a game of searching the illustrations to find the first letter of their names.

Last, Mrs. Greene wants to build into her read-aloud time to teach students about the sounds some letters make. While many of her students are still learning the names of the letters, Mrs. Greene decides that she will model this more advanced component of alphabet knowledge for her students. She makes a note to focus on the sound the letter *L* makes in the text, planning to pause when she reads a word that begins with the letter *L* and drag out the sound so that students can hear it. She also plans to call explicit attention to the sound the letter *L* makes and ask students to repeat the sound with her.

In Figure 6.4, Mrs. Greene has completed the planning column of the template. She notes the place in the book where she will address each of the four alphabet awareness skills. She also describes when she will engage students in each activity—before, during, or after reading. The next step is for Mrs. Greene to implement her plan in her kindergarten classroom. In the next section, we hear sample teacher talk as Mrs. Greene conducts a read-aloud of the alphabet book with her students.

Implementing the Reading

Incorporating activities that develop alphabet awareness into a read-aloud can be both quick and effective. It does not take prolonged attention to letters to be effective, nor is it desirable, since it would take too much time away from the cohesion and fluency of the reading itself. An exception would be if the book chosen for reading is an alphabet book. When reading an alphabet book as compared to a narrative book, a teacher may spend more time focused on building alphabet awareness simply because alphabet books take the letters as their primary content. We have seen a kindergarten teacher, Mrs. Greene, plan a read-aloud for the alphabet book *Alphabet Rescue* (Wood, 2006); below we describe what Mrs. Greene's read-aloud might sound like in the classroom.

Teacher Talk during Read-Alouds

Mrs. Greene calls children over to the brightly colored reading rug for the morning read-aloud. Once they are sitting comfortably, she smiles and welcomes them to the rug. Holding up the front cover of the book for children to see, she begins, "*Good morning. Today I am going to read a brand new book that our class has not read before. The title is* **Alphabet Rescue**. *It is by Audrey Wood and the pictures were drawn by Bruce Wood. We have been learning the letters of the alphabet, and this book is about an adventure those letters go on.*"

Opening the book to the front-end page, Mrs. Greene pauses. "*Wow! Look at that. This page looks like our alphabet strip at the front of the classroom. I can see all the letters we have been learning here. Can you see some letters you recognize? I am going to call Tony to come up and show us a letter he knows. Come on up, Tony.*"

Mrs. Greene holds the book up for the whole class to see as Tony searches the page for a letter he knows. He points to the letter *M* and says, "**M!**"

Mrs. Greene points to the letter *M* and responds, "*That's right, Tony! This is the letter M. High-five, Tony, for remembering the letter M! Tony, you can sit down now. I think we have time for someone else to have a turn. Linda, come on up and name a letter for us.*"

Linda walks to the front of the room to look at the alphabet on the page. She points to the letter *R* and says, "*Letter* **P.**"

Mrs. Greene responds, "*Oh, that is a good try, Linda, but this letter is the letter* **R.** *Can everyone see?*" Pointing to the letter *R*, Mrs. Greene asks, "*What letter?*" and waits for the class to respond chorally.

Ready to begin, Mrs. Greene turns the page and reads the first two pages of text. Then she pauses and says, "*The characters in our book are the little letters. Listen to the sound at the beginning of the words* **little** *and* **letters.**" Pointing to the letter *L* in the text, "*This is the letter L. What letter?*" Mrs. Greene pauses for students to repeat *L* and then continues, "*It makes the /l/ sound like in* **little** *and* **letters.** *Can you say 'luh'?*" After students have repeated the /l/ sound, Mrs. Greene says, "*The words* **lemon** *and* **lion** *and* **lunch** *all start with the letter L and the /l/ sound.*"

Mrs. Greene turns the page and continues to read the text. After reading the fourth page, Mrs. Greene states, "*I am looking for the letter F on this page because we have been talking about the letter F in our class.*" Mrs. Greene examines the page closely and then points to the letter *F*, "*Oh, here it is! I found the letter F. It is written in red right here. What letter is this?*" Mrs. Greene listens for the students' answers and then continues reading.

A few pages later, Mrs. Greene pauses after reading the text on the page. "*Look at all these colorful letters in this picture. It looks like the letters are very busy! Can you find any of the letters in your name in the picture? Raise your hand when you have found a letter from your name in the picture.*" Mrs. Greene calls on a student to come up to the book to point to a letter in his name. "*Owen, come on up and show us a letter that is in your name.*"

Owen points to the letter O and says, "*Here is my O.*"

"*That's right,*" says Mrs. Greene, pointing to the letter in the book. "*This is the letter O. Owen's name starts with the letter O. In this picture, the letter O is the color green.*"

Mrs. Greene returns to reading and then stops when she reads the phrase *little letters* in the text. "*Oh listen. **Little letters,**" dragging out the /l/ sound at the beginning of each word, "*Here is our L again making the /l/ sound. What letter makes the /l/ sound?*" Children respond, and Mrs. Greene reads on in the text.

On a page where the letter *B* is highlighted in red, Mrs. Greene calls a child up to identify the letter. "*I am looking for a special letter on this page. Nathanial, can you come up and find the letter B for us?*" Once Nathanial points to the letter on the page, Mrs. Greene turns to the whole class and asks, "*What letter did Nathanial find?*"

Mrs. Greene continues reading the rest of the book, pausing to ask children to identify specific letters in the text, to find any letter in their name in the illustrations, and to listen for the sound the letter *L* makes. At the end of the book, Mrs. Greene stops at the back-end page to allow two more students to come up and identify any letters they know.

Then Mrs. Greene concludes the read-aloud. "*Wow! We learned a lot about our little letters today. We saw some letters we remembered learning. We found some letters in our names. We even learned the /l/ sound that the L makes. You all did a great job thinking about letters today.*"

Reflecting on the Reading

After implementing her read-aloud in the classroom, Mrs. Greene sits down to reflect on the effectiveness of her alphabet awareness instruction. She uses the same template she used for planning, this time filling out the second and third columns. The second column asks her to reflect on how she did; to complete this column Mrs. Greene thinks about what she did and did not do related to her plan and also how the students responded to her instruction. The third column asks her to think about improving the read-aloud by setting some concrete goals for her next read-aloud focusing on alphabet awareness. Mrs. Greene's completed template is presented in Figure 6.5. Next we take a look at what Mrs. Greene's reflective process might be as she thinks through the strengths and challenges of her read-aloud.

A Focus on Alphabet Awareness in Read-Alouds

	Planning What is my plan?	Reflecting How did I do?	Goal Setting What will I do next time?
Identify Any Letter	I will pause when opening the book to the front-end page and call on one or two children to identify any letters they know on the page. I will repeat this after reading on the back-end page if there is time.	When I called Tony up to name a letter, I did not have the rest of the class participate in the activity like I did after Linda named a letter.	I will ask the rest of the class to repeat the name of the letter the student identifies so that the entire class benefits from the letter identification.
Identify Specific Letter/ Letters	Whenever I come to a page that has a letter highlighted in red, I will pause after reading and ask children to identify the specific letter highlighted.	I modeled finding F when highlighted in red. Looking back on it, I think that would have been a good time to ask students to find other F's on the page.	I will model identifying specific letters first and then offer students the opportunity to find the same letter on the page.
Identify a Letter in Child's Own Name	After every two or three pages, I will pause after reading and invite children to search the illustrations to find letters in their own names.	The students really loved this! All of the students wanted a turn, but I did not have enough time to let everyone point out a letter in their name.	I will warn students ahead of time that not everyone will have a turn, but I will put the book out during center time for students to mark "their" letters.
Sound–Symbol Correspondence	I will model the sound the letter L makes on page 2, saying the letter name and sound and asking students to repeat with me. Throughout the text I will drag out the sound the letter L makes.	Letter sounds are hard for my students. I talked about L and its sound whenever I read little letters. However, I don't think I consistently pointed to the letter L as I was saying its sound.	When working on letter sounds, I will remember to also call students' attention to the written letter so they can make the connection. I will point to the letter while making its sound.

FIGURE 6.5. Mrs. Greene's completed template.

Thinking about Strengths and Challenges

Overall, Mrs. Greene is pleased with the extent to which the alphabet activities she had planned for her read-aloud of *Alphabet Rescue* (Wood, 2006) engaged the students in thinking about the letters of the alphabet. She has rarely seen students so engaged in finding letters in a book; however, thinking back over the experience, she can also pinpoint several ways to improve her use of alphabet awareness activities during her next read-aloud.

Mrs. Greene planned to ask several children before and after reading to identify any letters they knew on the end pages of the book, where the entire alphabet is colorfully displayed. Before reading, Mrs. Greene called two students up to the book to name a letter. Tony pointed to the letter *M* and named it correctly right away; Linda pointed to the letter *R* and said "P." After Tony correctly identified his letter, Mrs. Greene remembers simply praising his success. After Linda's incorrect response, Mrs. Greene corrected her letter naming and engaged the entire class in saying the letter name together. Looking back at the experience for the whole class, Mrs. Greene realizes that Linda's mistake actually resulted in the whole class identifying a letter together, whereas her reaction to Tony's correct response did not similarly engage the other students. Therefore, Mrs. Greene decides to set a goal of always trying to get the entire class to name the letter after an individual student has done so either correctly or incorrectly. In this way, Mrs. Greene hopes that the whole class will benefit from additional practice at letter naming.

The second type of activity Mrs. Greene had planned was to identify specific letters when they were highlighted in red in the text. She knew the activity would be harder for students, so she began by modeling this letter identification with the letter *F* and then asked students to help her find specific letters that she named on other pages. Students definitely had more trouble finding specific letters when compared to the first activity of naming any letter they knew. Mrs. Greene thinks that she did not get the most out of her attempt at modeling the activity for students, because she expected them to identify different letters on subsequent pages while only modeling the letter *F*. Therefore, she concludes that a better activity would be to first model finding the specific letter and then asking individual students to find the same letter she found on the same page. So, for example, she may model finding the letter *T* on a page and then ask one or two students to come up and find additional letter *T*'s on the same page. In this way, Mrs. Greene will have modeled the activity first before asking students to hunt for the same letter.

Based on students' behavior and enthusiasm, Mrs. Greene concludes that students' favorite alphabet activity during the read-aloud was finding letters in their name in the illustrations. In fact, students enjoyed participating in this letter hunt so much that some students were disappointed when there was not enough time for them all to play. Mrs. Greene decides that next time she will warn students that not everyone will get a turn to point out a letter in their name during the read-aloud. Hopefully, warning students ahead of time will help ease their disappointment. Mrs. Greene also decides to continue students' enthusiasm with the activity after the read-aloud by giving students access to the book during center time. Mrs. Greene does not want the read-aloud itself to last too long but she does not want to stifle students' enthusiasm either, so she hopes that making the book available to students after the read-aloud will encourage students' thinking about the alphabet.

Last, Mrs. Greene introduced the harder concept of sound–symbol correspondence by drawing students' attention to the sound the letter *L* makes while reading. Mrs. Greene anticipated that this letter-sound activity would be the hardest concept for her students to understand since they are still learning letter names. However, she also knows that she must begin this instruction now to lay the groundwork for later phonemic awareness instruction. Therefore, Mrs. Greene decided to make this introductory letter-sound instruction very explicit—dragging out the sound the letter *L* makes whenever she read the alliterative phrase *little letters* in the text. Thinking back on this activity, Mrs. Greene determines that there is room for improvement. While she remembered to make the sound of the letter exaggerated while reading, she did not always bring students' attention to the corresponding written letter while making the sound. She realizes that students cannot make the connection between the letter and its sound if she does not emphasize both the sound of the letter and its corresponding written representation. Thus, her goal for the future is to always point to the letter as she makes its sound, a simple step with a potentially powerful effect for students' knowledge.

Closing Thoughts

Weaving alphabet awareness activities into a read-aloud is an effective way for building students' knowledge of the letters of the alphabet and their sounds. Alphabet picture books are especially useful for alphabet awareness instruction and come in a variety of forms. Research identifies four best practices for incorporating alphabet instruction into a read-aloud: (1) asking students to name any letter, (2) asking students to identify specific letters, (3) asking students to find letters in their names, and (4) making explicit the connection between letters and their sounds. The template for developing alphabet awareness in read-alouds is a tool for planning, reflecting on, and setting goals for future read-alouds. A blank planning template is presented in the Appendix for use in incorporating alphabet instruction during read-alouds.

CHAPTER 7

Developing Phonological Awareness through Read-Alouds

Let's focus on sounds! Phonological awareness is an understanding of the sounds in our language, whether large units like whole words or individual phoneme units like the sound /b/ (Snow, Burns, & Griffin, 1998; Yopp & Yopp, 2000). Phonological awareness instruction includes work at the word, syllable, onset–rime, and phoneme levels. When teachers ask students to think about words, to clap syllables, to generate rhyming words, or to blend the sounds in a word, they are targeting students' phonological awareness. Research suggests that a solid foundation in phonological awareness predicts future reading achievement (Ball & Blachman, 1988; NELP, 2007); therefore, fostering phonological awareness development is an important goal for early reading instruction. Luckily, the language of children's books provides a natural context in which teachers can embed phonological awareness instruction.

Planning the Reading

A teacher planning for phonological awareness instruction during read-alouds should consider the skill he or she wishes to target, the text that provides an opportunity for developing the skill, and the instructional activity that engages students to practice applying the skill. Phonological awareness skills appropriate for work with young students fall into four categories: (1) word awareness, (2) syllable awareness, (3) rhyming, and (4) sound awareness. A student with word awareness understands that oral speech is made up of units called words. When a teacher asks students to count the number of words in a sentence, he or she is targeting word awareness. Similarly, syllable awareness is the knowledge that words are made up of smaller units called syllables. Often, teachers will ask students to segment words into syllables by clapping in order to help students hear the syllables in words. Rhyming words sound the same at the end. Teachers can target rhyming by asking students to listen for rhyming words in stories. Sound awareness, or phoneme awareness, involves hearing the individual sounds in words. For example, a student who can identify three sounds—/c/ /a/ /t/—in the word *cat* has sound awareness. A teacher working with young students can begin initial sound awareness instruction by targeting initial sounds in words. Depending on the level of phonological awareness students possess, a teacher can target one or multiple phonological awareness skills in the same read-aloud. After determining the phonological awareness skill or skills for instruction, a teacher should then find a book that provides opportunities for developing the skill.

Matching a Book to the Skill

Let's play with sound. A read-aloud that develops children's phonological awareness is one in which you and your children are enjoying the sounds of the English language. You may call your students' attention to rhyming words, words that begin with the same sound, or the individual sounds they hear in words. Read-alouds that focus on phonological awareness also connect well with alphabet instruction, as children can begin to hear the sounds of letters they are learning during other parts of the classroom day.

You probably already have a collection of great books that target phonological awareness instruction in your classroom library. If not, it is easy to find high-quality

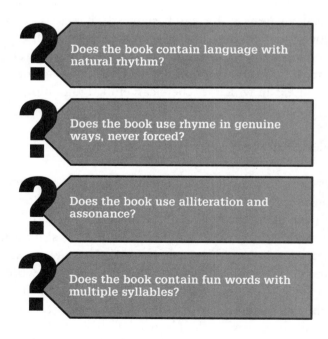

FIGURE 7.1. Characteristics of books that develop phonological awareness.

children's books that can be used for phonological awareness instruction. We look for books that have the characteristics listed in Figure 7.1.

First, look for books that have natural rhythm. Books with natural rhythm when read aloud should sound almost musical. Many books that target phonological awareness rhyme. There is no shortage of children's books that rhyme; however, not all rhyming books are created equal. We have all read books in which the rhyme is so forced that it feels choppy or stilted as we read. Good rhyming books use rhyme when it works, never forcing words into awkward rhymes. Books that use alliteration or assonance can be especially helpful when targeting phonological awareness. Many alphabet books include alliteration in their structure for teaching the alphabet and can work nicely for talking about words with the same beginning sounds too. Finally, books with fun, unusual words with multiple syllables are great when drawing children's attention to the number of syllables in words. Poetry often includes all of these characteristics and, therefore, can work especially well for phonological awareness instruction. We have included in Figure 7.2 a list of both books and children's poetry anthologies that you may consider adding to your collection.

Storybooks
There Was an Old Lady Who Swallowed a Fly by Pam Adams (2007)
Giraffes Can't Dance by Giles Andreae (1999)
Llama Llama Mad at Mama by Anna Dewdney (2007)
The Snail and the Whale by Julia Donaldson (2004)
Alligator Arrived with Apples: A Potluck Alphabet Feast by Crescent Dragonwagon (1992)
In the Tall, Tall Grass by Denise Fleming (1991)
One Fish Two Fish Red Fish Blue Fish by Dr. Seuss (1960)
Baseball Hour by Carol Nevius (2008)
Piggies in the Pumpkin Patch by Mary Peterson and Jennifer Rofe (2010)
All the World by Liz Garton Scanlon (2009)
Walter Was Worried by Laura Vaccaro Seeger (2006)
Sheep in a Jeep by Nancy Shaw (2006)
Silly Sally by Audrey Wood (2007)
How Do Dinosaurs Eat Their Food? by Jane Yolen (2005)
Poetry Anthologies
Miss Mary Mack and Other Children's Street Rhymes by Joanna Cole and Stephanie Calmenson (1990)
Revolting Rhymes by Roald Dahl (1982)
Favorite Nursery Rhymes from Mother Goose by Scott Gustafson (2007)
Be Glad Your Nose Is on Your Face and Other Poems by Jack Prelutsky (2008)
Where the Sidewalk Ends by Shel Silverstein (2004)

FIGURE 7.2. Books on our shelves to develop phonological awareness.

Deciding How to Develop the Skill

Once a book has been chosen for a read-aloud targeting phonological awareness, you must determine how to develop the skill. Research describes instructional activities for each of the four categories of phonological awareness: (1) word awareness, (2) syllable awareness, (3) rhyme, and (4) sound awareness. Figure 7.3 summarizes the best practices for developing phonological awareness in the context of read-alouds.

To foster students' word awareness, you can ask students to count the number of words in a sentence (Adams, 1990; Justice, Kaderavek, Bowles, & Grimm, 2005). During reading, you may pause on a page to model or ask students independently to physically represent each word in a sentence through a repetitive movement, such as clapping, tapping, or snapping. Once students have physically represented the words in a sentence, ask them to count the number of words by counting the number of times they clapped, tapped, or snapped. For example, you might say, "Let's clap the number of words in the sentence *The cat sat on the mat.*" After clapping with students, you can call attention to the purpose of clapping by saying, "Good. How many words did we hear in that sentence? How many times did we clap?"

Syllable awareness activities include segmenting (Adams, 1990; Justice, Kaderavek, et al., 2005) and blending (Adams, 1990; Yopp & Yopp, 2000) syllables in words. Teachers ask students to segment syllables when they ask them to break a word into syllables and count them. You may say something like, "Let's clap out the number of syllables we hear in the word *elephant.*" Clapping together with students, you would chant, "*El-e-phant,*" and ask, "How many sounds did we hear?" To blend syllables, you may introduce the concept by saying, "We can pull sounds and

Best Practice	Description
Counting words	Model and/or invite children to clap, tap, or snap words in a sentence and ask how many words they heard.
Segmenting syllables	Model and/or invite children to segment the syllables in a word and count them.
Blending syllables	Model and/or invite children to blend the segmented syllables of a word.
Rhyme identification	Draw attention to the rhyming words and ask students what they notice about the words or have them identify a set of rhyming words just read.
Rhyme completion	Leave off the last word of a sentence that requires children to fill in a possible rhyming word and discusses the pair of rhyming words.
Rhyme production	Model and/or invite children to produce rhyming words and then record in writing on a chart.
Alliteration/initial sound identification	Focus on beginning sounds by drawing attention to words that have the same beginning sounds.

FIGURE 7.3. Best practices in phonological awareness.

words apart and put them back together. Listen . . . *el-e-phant*. Now I am going to put it back together by saying the syllables faster . . . *elephant*." Once your students are familiar with blending, you may change your directions to say, "I am going to pull sounds apart in a word and say them slowly. I want you to put it back together. *El-e-phant*. What word?"

Rhyme activities during read-alouds can include rhyme identification, rhyme completion, and rhyme production. Rhyme identification occurs when you draw students' attention to rhyming words or asks students to identify rhyming words in the text (Richgels, 1995; Yopp & Yopp, 2000). For example, you may provide rhyming words for children to consider by asking, "What do you notice about the words *rat* and *bat*?" Or, you may ask children to identify the rhyming words in the text, "Who can tell me two words that rhyme in the sentence I just read?" Rhyme completion tasks require students to fill in a possible rhyming word to complete a sentence started by the teacher (Neuman et al., 2000; Richgels, 1995; Yopp & Yopp, 2000). You may begin the sentence, "She wants to run outside and play on this bright and beautiful sunny _____," leaving the last word out for students to supply. A child may respond, "Day," to which you could comment, "Yes, you helped me complete the sentence with a rhyming word. Our rhyming words are *play* and *day*." Last, rhyme production tasks ask children to produce rhyming words (Adams, 1990; Justice, Kaderavek, et al., 2005; McGee & Purcell-Gates, 1997). During your read-aloud, you may pause and ask children to brainstorm a list of rhyming words, which you can record in writing. You may ask, "Can you think of any words that might rhyme with the word *sun*? Let's write them down on our chalkboard."

The hardest phonological awareness skill for young students is sound awareness. To foster students' beginning sound awareness, focus on the beginning sounds of words by drawing students' attention to words that begin with the same sounds (Adams, 1990; McFadden, 1998). Finding an alliterative phrase in a book, you may pause and say, "*Silly Sally*. What do you notice about those two words? That's right, they both have the same beginning sound! Let's make that sound together." You may even expand the activity by asking students whether they can think of other words that begin with the same sound.

Planning Template

In this section, we present the planning template for developing children's phonological awareness (see Figure 7.4). The template lists the best practices discussed above in the first column, and then provides room for you to plan how to incorporate the best practices in your read-alouds, reflect on how your phonological awareness instruction went, and set goals for improving future read-alouds targeting phonological awareness. A blank version of the template is available in the Appendix (Form 5).

To illustrate using the planning template for phonological awareness, we describe Mr. Ruble, a reading specialist working with the first-grade team at an urban elementary school. Mr. Ruble has been teaching elementary students for 10 years. His

A Focus on Phonological Awareness in Read-Alouds

	Planning What is my plan?	Reflecting How did I do?	Goal Setting What will I do next time?
Counting Words	I will model counting the number of words in the first sentence of the story by clapping each word. Then I will ask children to clap and count the number of words in the second sentence with me.		
Segmenting Syllables	I will model breaking apart syllables in words by choosing a few good words from the story—llama, puzzles—and then invite children to count the syllables with me.		
Blending Syllables	For all the words I break apart, I will then model blending the syllables back together. I will ask children to help me blend the syllables back together into words.		
Rhyme Identification	I will read the title of the book and ask children what they notice about the words in the title. I will ask children to listen for rhyming words.		
Rhyme Completion	After reading half of the book, I will see if children can complete some of the familiar rhyming phrases by leaving off the last rhyming word.		
Rhyme Production	At the end of the read-aloud I will ask children to help me brainstorm some words that rhyme with the word play from the story. I will record our list on the dry-erase board.		
Alliteration/ Initial Sound Identification	During reading, I will call students' attention to pairs of words that begin with the same sound, such as mad and Mama; big and buildings; and llama, like, and lunch.		

FIGURE 7.4. Mr. Ruble's initial planning template.

school is located in an urban community, right across the street from an apartment complex with a predominantly Spanish-speaking population. This year Mr. Ruble is working in one classroom with 23 first graders who are all learning English as a second language. In order to meet his reading goals for the end of first grade, Mr. Ruble knows that he must accelerate the reading development of his students and must quickly develop a solid foundation of prerequisite reading skills so that his students can succeed at decoding and word identification later in the year. Thus, he begins the school year by focusing on phonological awareness.

Within the first month of the new school year the first-grade team at Mr. Ruble's school works on a unit about emotions as they strive to develop positive expectations and behavior management routines for the classroom. To fit within this theme, Mr. Ruble chooses Anna Dewdney's *Llama Llama Mad at Mama* (2007) as a whole-group read-aloud during his in-class reading intervention. In the story the young llama behaves poorly when out shopping with his mother and must learn to regulate his behavior even when doing something he does not enjoy. Mr. Ruble likes the book for targeting phonological awareness because of its rhyming structure and use of alliteration. In addition, the book includes colorful illustrations, depicting the emotions of the characters, and a realistic story line to which many young students can relate.

When planning his read-aloud, Mr. Ruble uses the planning template to think about how to use the book to develop important phonological awareness skills. Mr. Ruble's completed planning template is presented in Figure 7.5. First, Mr. Ruble decides to include a range of phonological awareness skills that focus on word, syllable, rhyme, and sound awareness. He anticipates that students in his classroom will need to focus on different levels within phonological awareness and by including skills at multiple levels in the read-aloud he will ensure that he is meeting the needs of all students. To that end, he begins thinking about including one episode of modeling and inviting children to participate in an activity at the easiest level of phonological awareness—word awareness. He decides to model this activity early on in the read-aloud as a warm-up for students who have already mastered this skill and as a review and opportunity for practice for the very few students who are still trying to master the concept. Therefore, he plans to read the first page of the story and then to pause and model clapping and counting the number of words in the first sentence. Directly after modeling the skill, he will invite the students to help him clap and count the number of words in the second sentence. Since this activity targets the most basic word-awareness level of phonological awareness, which almost all of his students have mastered, he plans to target the skill one time during the read-aloud.

Based on assessment data, Mr. Ruble knows that several of his students are still struggling with segmenting and blending syllables in words. He decides that he will model counting the number of syllables in several words in the book on the first few pages and then invite children to help him count syllables. He also decides to combine segmenting and blending syllables since they are complementary skills. He thinks that it may be confusing for some children to clap the number of words in a sentence and to clap the number of syllables in words, so he will model tapping out the number of syllables on his fingers instead of clapping during this read-aloud. He chooses words with varying number of syllables, so that children can practice with both shorter and longer words.

Mr. Ruble has been working on rhyming words with students since the beginning of the year. He has read rhyming books and poems and engaged students in rhyming activities in both whole-group and small-group instruction during the reading block. He, therefore, hopes that students will be able to recognize that he will be reading a rhyming book once they have heard the title. He decides to read the title and then to pause and ask students if they notice anything special about the words in the title. Once students have identified that the words rhyme in the title, he will ask them to listen for other rhyming words while he is reading the book.

One of the reasons Mr. Ruble chose *Llama Llama Mad at Mama* (Dewdney, 2007) for a read-aloud is its rhyming structure and repetition of rhyming words with the same ending. Mr. Ruble hopes that the repetition of words that rhyme with *llama* throughout the book will help students predict new rhyming words. He plans to engage students in generating rhyming words by asking them to predict the rhyming word that completes a sentence from the book when he leaves out the ending rhyme. This strategy will allow students to practice generating rhyming words with support from the text.

As a final practice with rhyme, Mr. Ruble will ask students to apply their knowledge of rhyming words to a task after reading. He will choose the word *play* from the book and ask children to think of as many words as they can that rhyme with it. He will record their responses on his dry-erase board in the classroom and underline the ending parts of the words as extra emphasis that they rhyme. Mr. Ruble plans to call on some children first who he thinks understand rhyme to serve as good peer models. Once he has several rhyming examples on the board, Mr. Ruble will call on other students to name a rhyming word. If a student names a word that does not rhyme, he will be able to write the word on the board, underline the ending, and then compare it to the endings of words that do rhyme to see whether the class can determine that the word does not rhyme and the reason why.

Just as many of the rhyming words are repeated throughout the book, the same beginning sounds are also used in alliterative phrases. The /m/ sound repeats in the title, *Mad at Mama*. The /b/ sound repeats in *big buildings*, and the /l/ sound repeats in the question *What would llama like for lunch?* Mr. Ruble knows that while many of his students still struggle with rhyme, a very small number are ready for the challenge of sound awareness, the hardest level of phonological awareness and a stepping stone toward decoding. Since this is the first time Mr. Ruble will introduce listening for words that begin with the same sound, he will exclusively model and call students' attention to this concept in the read-aloud without expecting students to generate alliteration on their own this time.

After planning which phonological awareness skills he will incorporate into his read-aloud, how he will engage students in thinking about each skill, and where—before, during, or after—in the read-aloud he will complete the activities, Mr. Ruble is ready to implement his plan. In the next section we hear a portion of Mr. Ruble's read-aloud with his students as he works to foster their phonological awareness development.

Implementing the Reading

Mr. Ruble enjoys talking with students about phonological awareness in the context of read-alouds. He introduces word, syllable, rhyme, and sound awareness in whole-group instruction through modeling and discussing with students; however, he finds that students really become engaged when he asks them to apply what they know about phonological awareness while he is reading them a good book. Keeping track of students' responses during the read-aloud also provides Mr. Ruble with important information about which students have mastered the concept, which students need more practice, and which students need more intensive instruction in small-group settings. In the next section we describe what Mr. Ruble's read-aloud might sound like when he focuses on phonological awareness.

Teacher Talk during Read-Alouds

Mr. Ruble calls students over to the rug for his daily read-aloud. *"Row one, push seats in and show me that you are ready. Row two, push seats in and show me that you are ready to listen to our story reading. Row three, push seats in and join us on the rug."* Since it is near the beginning of the year, Mr. Ruble reminds students about expected behavior during reading before he begins his read-aloud. *"Everyone, remember when we are participating in a read-aloud we need to be respectful by not talking while I am reading or when another student is responding to a question. Now, let's get started."* Mr. Ruble begins, *"I have a great book for us to read together today! Listen to the title—Llama Llama Mad at Mama. Does anyone notice anything about the words in the title? Listen again as I read it to you,* **Llama Llama Mad at Mama.***"*

Mr. Ruble calls on a student who raises her hand; the student responds, *"Rhyme."*

"That's right, Julia, the words **llama** *and* **mama** *rhyme. They sound the same at the end. We are going to be reading a rhyming book today. As I read, I want you to listen for words that rhyme. Did you hear anything else special in the title? Listen again:* **Llama Llama Mad at Mama.***"* This time as Mr. Ruble reads the title, he emphasizes the /m/ sound at the beginning of the words *mad* and *mama*. A few students catch on and raise their hands enthusiastically. Mr. Ruble calls on Juan, who makes the /m/ sound. *"Juan is making the /m/ sound for the letter* **M.** *He heard the same /m/ sound at the beginning of the words* **mad** *and* **Mama.** *As I read, I want you to also listen for words that sound the same at the beginning."* Mr. Ruble opens the book and begins to read.

After the first page, Mr. Ruble pauses and models counting the number of words in the first sentence: "*I just read two sentences on this page. I would like you to watch and listen as I count the number of words in the first sentence. I am going to clap to help me count.*" Rereading the first sentence, Mr. Ruble claps once for each word in the sentence. "**Llama**," clap. "**Llama**," clap. "**Having**," clap. "**Fun**," clap. "*I clapped four times; one clap for each word in the sentence, so there are four words in this sentence. Let's do the next sentence together. Remember to clap once for each word.*" Mr. Ruble rereads the second sentence, clapping along with the students. "**Blocks**," clap. "**And**," clap. "**Puzzles**," clap. "**In**," clap. "**The**," clap. "**Sun**," clap. "*Wow, that was a lot of claps! How many times did we clap, Maria?*"

"*Six!*"

"*That's right, Maria, we clapped six times—one clap for each word in the sentence. Okay, let's keep reading.*" Mr. Ruble continues reading the book enthusiastically, raising and lowering his voice when appropriate and adding expression to engage his audience in the reading. He pauses when he comes to two or three interesting words to give students practice with breaking words into syllables and then blending them back together. "*Boys and girls, let's look at the word **dreaming**. Listen as I break that word apart into syllables: **dream-ing**. I can hear two parts in that word: **dream-ing**. There are two syllables. I can also put those syllables back together to create one word: **dream-ing**, **dream-ing**, **dreaming**.*"

Mr. Ruble continues reading, briefly pausing to call attention to words that begin with the same sound. "*Wow, did you hear that? Let's read that again: **What would llama like for lunch**? Did you hear the /l/ sound at the beginning of the words **llama, like**, and **lunch**? Those words start with the same /l/ sound.*"

About halfway through the reading, Mr. Ruble decides to see whether children are catching on to the rhyming structure in the text by leaving off the last word in the sentence for students to complete. Mr. Ruble reads a sentence, "*I think shopping's boring, too—but at least I'm here with _____,*" and then pauses to see how students respond. When no students respond, Mr. Ruble prompts, "*What word do you think fits there?*" and rereads the sentence. A student gasps and raises his hand. Mr. Ruble calls, "*Hector, what do you think?*"

"*Too!*"

"*Well, that is a good try. The word **too** is in the first part of the sentence, what word might rhyme with **too** that makes sense in this sentence?*" When no students respond, Mr. Ruble continues, "*I'm here with you,*" emphasizing the word *you*. "*Too and **you** rhyme!*"

Mr. Ruble finishes reading the rest of the book, weaving in opportunities for students to break and blend syllables and calling attention to rhyming words and words that begin with same sound. After reading, he engages students in one last rhyming activity. "*We listened for rhyming words in the book today. Rhyming words are words that sound the same. I have a challenge for you since you were so good at listening for rhyming words today. Let's see if you can think of words that rhyme with the word **play**.*" Mr. Ruble writes the word *play* at the top of his dry-erase easel. "*Who can tell me a word that rhymes with **play**?*"

When none of his students respond, Mr. Ruble provides a hint, "*You can feed a horse _____.*"

A student calls out, "*Hay!*"

"*That's right, hay and play rhyme.*" Mr. Ruble writes the word *hay* under the word *play* and underlines the *ay* at the end of each word. "*How about today is Mon-_____?*"

"*Day!*" several children call out together.

"*Yes, play and day rhyme too. They sound the same. Any other words you can think of that rhyme with play? We have hay and play, day and play. How about, Arielle, when you get tired you can _____ down to rest.*"

Arielle responds, "*Lay.*"

"*Yes, you can lay down to rest. Lay and play rhyme too! See how they have the same ending?*" Mr. Ruble writes the word *lay* in his list of rhyming words and underlines the ending. "*Okay, guys, you have done a great job thinking of words that rhyme with the word play. Let's reread our rhyming words: play, hay, day, and lay. They all end with the ay sound. Good work!*"

Reflecting on the Reading

As the reading specialist, Mr. Ruble has time back in his office to reflect on the read-aloud. He uses his planning template to review and compare what he had planned to do with what actually happened during the read-aloud. He uses the template to record notes about the strengths of his read-aloud and those activities that students seemed to struggle with. Taking into account students' response to the phonological awareness activities in this read-aloud, Mr. Ruble sets goals for the types and extent of activities he will include in his next read-aloud with these students. Mr. Ruble's completed template is presented in Figure 7.5. In the next section we discuss what Mr. Ruble considers to be the strengths and challenges of his read-aloud.

Thinking about Strengths and Challenges

Looking back over his read-aloud, Mr. Ruble can easily distinguish which phonological awareness skills his students seem to understand and which skills challenged them. He was satisfied with his students' ability to count the number of words in a sentence. He modeled this skill first and then asked his students to clap and count with him, an activity that all of the students did successfully. As a result, Mr. Ruble plans to focus less on this skill in future read-alouds, saving time to devote to conceptually harder phonological awareness skills. Because he thinks his students have mastered this skill, when he does incorporate it in future read-alouds he will not model it first but simply ask students to demonstrate the skill.

A Focus on Phonological Awareness in Read-Alouds

	Planning What is my plan?	Reflecting How did I do?	Goal Setting What will I do next time?
Counting Words	I will model counting the number of words in the first sentence of the story by clapping each word. Then I will ask children to clap and count the number of words in the second sentence with me.	I followed my plan and modeled first and then asked students to clap and count with me. The students were very successful with this task.	I think all of my students have mastered this basic-level activity. I think I will phase out this activity to concentrate more time during reading to other, harder tasks.
Segmenting Syllables	I will model breaking apart syllables in words by choosing a few good words from the story—llama, puzzles—and then invite children to count the syllables with me.	I realized after reading that all of the words I chose were two-syllable words.	Next time I will choose one-, two-, and three-syllable words from the text to break apart so that students can practice with different words.
Blending Syllables	For all the words I break apart, I will then model blending the syllables back together. I will ask children to help me blend the syllables back together into words.	Students had no trouble blending the syllables back together, but it may be that it was because they had just broken the word apart.	Next time I will separate the two skills of blending and segmenting by using different words to see if students are really understanding the idea.
Rhyme Identification	I will read the title of the book and ask children what they notice about the words in the title. I will ask children to listen for rhyming words.	I asked students to listen for rhyming words but I had no system for checking whether they heard them.	I think I will ask children to tug their ears or put their finger on their nose when they hear rhyming words in the text.
Rhyme Completion	After reading half of the book, I will see if children can complete some of the familiar rhyming phrases by omitting the last rhyming word.	I expected students to catch on to what I was asking them to do, but they did not. Then they had trouble filling in the rhyming words.	I will provide clearer directions that I want them to fill in a rhyming word. I will also choose sentences with concrete, familiar words.
Rhyme Production	At the end of the read-aloud I will ask children to help me brainstorm some words that rhyme with the word play from the story. I will record our list on the dry-erase board.	This was hard for students! When students did not respond readily, I provided them with several prompts to help them think of words that rhyme with the word play.	I will definitely repeat this activity. I will choose a word with a better ending so that children may know more words that rhyme. Words like cat or frog may be good ones to start with.
Alliteration/ Initial Sound Identification	During reading, I will call students' attention to pairs of words that begin with the same sound, such as mad and Mama; big and buildings; and llama, like, and lunch.	I really emphasized the beginning sounds in phrases that used alliteration. I modeled hearing the sounds, trying to call attention to the idea.	As students progress with hearing the initial sounds in words, I will repeat this activity more frequently.

FIGURE 7.5. Mr. Ruble's completed template.

Mr. Ruble planned to target students' syllable awareness by pausing after reading a word to allow students time to segment the syllables and then to blend the syllables back together into the word. He planned to repeat this activity several times during the entire read-aloud with different words. After the read-aloud, Mr. Ruble realized that he had inadvertently only chosen two-syllable words for students to practice. He considers this a major oversight on his part and plans to remedy this by incorporating words with one, two, and three syllables in his very next read-aloud with these students. He also reconsiders his decision to have students segment and blend the same words. While he thinks this was a useful way to model the skills, he is concerned that students may have had too much support with the blending task because they had just segmented the exact same word. Next time he plans to choose different words for segmenting and blending so that students have the opportunity to practice the skills separately. He thinks it is important to know whether students can blend syllables into words that they have not heard as a whole word first.

Mr. Ruble incorporated three activities that focused on rhyme into his read-aloud. For rhyme identification, he used the title of the book to see whether children could recognize that he was going to read a rhyming book. Mr. Ruble was pleased that one of his students noticed right away that the title rhymes. Once students understood that he was going to read a rhyming book, Mr. Ruble asked them to listen for rhyming words while he read. However, Mr. Ruble reflected after his read-aloud that he did not have a good system in place for recognizing when students heard rhyming words. He decided that in the future he would ask students to do some physical action, like put their hands on their head or their fingers on their ears, when they hear a rhyme. Mr. Ruble hopes that this physical reminder will help him monitor when students are hearing and identifying rhyme.

Mr. Ruble also asked students to complete rhyming sentences when he left off the second rhyming word. He thought that his students would understand this task after hearing about half of the book; however, students seemed to be uncertain about what he wanted them to do. Mr. Ruble decides to provide clearer directions about the task before he omits words for students to fill in during future read-alouds. He also considers using sentences that contain more concrete words. He thinks that students will be able to predict rhyming words better if they are concrete objects with which students are familiar. Mr. Ruble thinks it would really be great too if the objects were represented in the illustrations of the book, giving students another scaffold for completing the rhyme with a word that makes sense in the story.

As a final rhyming task, Mr. Ruble asked students to generate words on their own that rhyme with the word *play*. Mr. Ruble discovered that this task was extremely hard for his students. In fact, they were unable to come up with rhyming words on their own. When Mr. Ruble provided some prompts for words that rhymed with *play*, such as a hint about horses eating *hay*, students were then able to brainstorm some rhyming words. Mr. Ruble sees from this read-aloud that his students need a lot more practice with thinking of their own rhyming words. He plans to repeat this activity after future read-alouds. He also thinks he will begin by choosing a word from a very common short-vowel word family, such as *at* or *og*. Mr. Ruble predicts that students will be able to think of more words on their own that rhyme with words like *cat* or *frog*.

Finally, Mr. Ruble introduced the concept of initial sound identification by emphasizing the beginning sounds of words in alliterative phrases. For example, he emphasized the /l/ sound at the beginning of the words *llama*, *like*, and *lunch*. His goal for this read-aloud was simply to call students' attention to the fact that these words started with the same sound. Mr. Ruble knows that sound awareness is the hardest level of phonological awareness and that many of his students are just not yet ready to identify initial sounds on their own. He will continue to model this skill in future read-alouds, and as students begin to recognize when words sound the same at the beginning he will ask them to identify alliteration in books with less modeling from him.

Closing Thoughts

Phonological awareness is an important building block for future reading success. Reading aloud is a great context for incorporating phonological awareness activities in fun and engaging ways for young students. Research indicates several best practices for developing phonological awareness during read-alouds, including (1) word counting, (2) syllable segmenting, (3) syllable blending, (4) rhyme identification, (5) rhyme completion, (6) rhyme production, and (7) initial sound identification. A single read-aloud can target phonological awareness skills at each of the four levels of difficulty: word awareness, syllable awareness, rhyming, and sound awareness. By including a range of phonological awareness activities within a single read-aloud, you can successfully target the unique needs of individual students.

CHAPTER 8

Developing Comprehension through Read-Alouds

Comprehension is the essence of reading instruction. The ultimate goal of teaching all the skills discussed previously in this book is to support students in processing text and being able to extract and construct information within and across texts (Dole, Duffy, Roehler, & Pearson, 1991; National Institute of Child Health and Human Development, 2000; Snow, 2002). Even young children who cannot yet read can begin to develop foundational comprehension skills, such as predicting what a book will be about or making connections between a book and personal experience, while listening and discussing a book during a read-aloud.

Planning the Reading

When planning to target comprehension during read-alouds, consider how to make the process of applying strategies and skills visible to children as well as how to scaffold the children's ability to think critically. This scaffold will take place during your discussions and sharing of information with your students; the time where your students as learners will engage in thinking and talking about the content of the book you read. It will be through these sharing moments that your students will be involved in thinking and problem-solving processes. Therefore, we advocate for many opportunities for discussion, allowing students not only to show their knowledge but also expand their thinking.

Matching a Book to the Skill

There are many books that may be appropriate to use in a read-aloud focused on reading comprehension. To narrow your search, consider the age of your students, their interests, and the content of the book, as well as instructional applications and implications. At the same time keep in mind the students' performance as informed by assessment measures and your grade-level expectations.

In terms of developing comprehension skills, we have identified some specific text elements that can support your instruction. Figure 8.1 includes a list of these criteria that you can use when considering books for comprehension instruction.

During your instruction you will need to support your students as critical readers who are able to "read" the clues that a book gives them. Such clues can come from the words as well as the artwork. Therefore, one of the first elements you can look for is clear and supportive artwork. Clear pictures that expand or support the meaning of the words in the text can become clues that the students will use to predict what will follow. In addition, clear artwork, even if it contradicts the text, will engage them in discussions on the development of illusive meanings and false predictions when relying only on the artwork. When reading nonfiction texts, photographs will not only engage your students but will also give them a clear idea of what the author describes.

A second characteristic is descriptive language. While listening to a story being read, students develop a visual image of the characters and their problems. When a book describes the character and uses vivid words about his or her actions or emotions, it assists the students in better understanding the intentions of the character

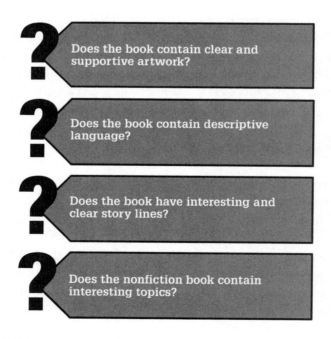

FIGURE 8.1. Criteria for books that support comprehension.

and his or her actions. Dialogue allows students to view the interactions of the characters and evaluate their personalities. Descriptive language that elaborates on settings, characters, and problems, or that provides details on a topic, has the potential of assisting students while they make sense of the read-aloud and attempt to understand your thinking about how you reached a conclusion.

In fiction texts, look for interesting and clear story lines. When the story line is clear, the students can mentally sort the information they hear in the beginning, middle, and end. While listening, they can develop a mental representation of the characters—their actions, problems, efforts to solve their problems—and the solution. A clear story line will assist the students when they are asked to retrieve the information and retell the content of the book or an isolated section such as the solution of a problem. The component of interest is related to the engagement of your students to the story. An interesting story line is one in which there is adventure and efforts by the characters to resolve a challenge. An interesting story line does not necessarily involve the presence of more than one problem that a character tries to solve. It relates more to the appropriateness of the content and its ability to relate to your audience's interests.

Consider including nonfiction texts in your read-alouds. Students are truly excited to learn about subjects and themes that are part of the real world, and reading nonfiction is an excellent way to fuel this interest. Nonfiction texts have a different structure than fiction. There is no story line, but the information has a specific structure that accomplishes a specific purpose. For example, the purpose may be to compare and contrast, classify, or show a procedure. Within this complexity, these books lend themselves to learning as your students gain real information about facts on a variety of topics. This information, though, should be engaging and such that will peak the interest of your students, who hopefully will want to read and learn more on the topic. Therefore, look for topics that are interesting and can expand into other activities in your classroom.

In Figure 8.2, we provide you with a list of fiction and nonfiction books we like to read when focusing on children's comprehension development. Some of these books may already be on your bookshelves; if not, consider them as representative fiction and nonfiction texts that can support reading comprehension instruction.

Deciding How to Develop the Skill

Comprehension refers to the ability of a reader to make sense of a text. To help young readers develop beginning comprehension, teachers can focus on modeling and engaging students in practicing comprehension skills and strategies. The selection of these skills and strategies is not random. On the contrary, there is thoughtful and deliberate investigation of what works. In the following section we provide approaches that are based on scientifically based reading research, research that suggests the approaches support young children's comprehension development (Pressley & Hilden, 2002). These procedures are based on asking questions. Questioning

Fiction Selection	Nonfiction Selection
The Hello, Goodbye Window by Norton Juster (2005)	*Owen and Mzee: The True Story of a Remarkable Friendship* by Isabella Hatkoff, Craig Hatkoff, and Dr. Paula Kahumbu (2006)
Lilly's Purple Plastic Purse by Kevin Henkes (1996)	
The Relatives Came by Cynthia Rylant (1985)	*Looking for Miza: The True Story of the Mountain Gorilla Family Who Rescued One of Their Own* by Craig Hatkoff, Juliana Hatkoff, Isabella Hatkoff, and Dr. Paula Kahumbu (2008)
Stephanie's Ponytail by Robert Munsch (1996)	
Knuffle Bunny: A Cautionary Tale by Mo Willems (2004)	
Strega Nona: An Old Tale by Tomie dePaola (1975)	*Knut: How One Little Polar Bear Captivated the World* by Craig Hatkoff, Juliana Hatkoff, Isabella Hatkoff, and Dr. Gerald Uhlich (2007)
David Goes to School by David Shannon (1999)	
The Snowy Day by Ezra Jack Keats (2006)	
Wemberly Worried by Kevin Henkes (2000)	*Time for Kids: Spiders!* by Nicole Iorio (2005b)
The Pigeon Has Feelings Too!: A Smidgeon of Pigeon by Mo Willems (2005)	*Owen and Mzee: A Day Together* by Isabella Hatkoff, Craig Hatkoff, and Dr. Paula Kahumbu (2008)
Crow Boy by Taro Yashima (1955)	*Winter's Tail: How One Little Dolphin Learned to Swim Again* by Julianna Hatkoff, Isabella Hatkoff, and Craig Hatkoff (2009)
Thank You, Mr. Falker by Patricia Polacco (1998)	
The Little Engine That Could by Wally Piper (2005)	*When I Was Young in the Mountains* by Cynthia Rylant (1982)
Don't Let the Pigeon Drive the Bus by Mo Williams (2003)	
If You Take a Mouse to the Movies by Laura Numeroff (2000)	*If You Lived in Colonial Times* by Ann McGovern and June Otani (1992)
Ox-Cart Man by Donald Hall (1979)	*Owen and Mzee: The Language of Friendship* by Isabella Hatkoff, Craig Hatkoff, and Dr. Paula Kahumbu (2007)
	If Your Name Was Changed at Ellis Island by Ellen Levine (1993)
	Animals Nobody Loves by Seymour Simon (2008)
	Zipping, Zapping, Zooming Bats by Ann Earle (1995)
	Time for Kids: Bats! by Nicole Iorio (2005a)
	Why Mosquitoes Buzz in People's Ears: A West African Tale by Verna Aardema (1975)
	Why Don't Elephants Live in the City? by Katherine Smith (2004)
	Frogs by Elizabeth Carney (2009)

FIGURE 8.2. Books on our shelves to develop comprehension.

can support classroom discussions and also give you an opportunity to intervene and make the meaning-making process visible through thinking aloud. Consider all these practices opportunities for discovery as you discover what your students can and cannot do. There are several types of questions you can ask young students to develop comprehension. Figure 8.3 contains a summary of the types of questions that can go far toward growing children's comprehension.

Prediction as a comprehension strategy has many benefits for the reader (Wasik & Bond, 2001; Wasik et al., 2006). Through prediction, students use clues from the

Strategy	Questions
Prediction Questions	What is the title of the book? What is the picture? What do you know about them? Based on this knowledge, what do you think will happen? What did we learn so far? Was the prediction correct? Why? What will happen next?
Open-Ended Questions	How did you . . . ? Why was the character . . . ?
Text-to-Self Connection Questions	How did the character react? Have you reacted in that way? Have you ever . . . ?
Text-to-Text Connection Questions	How are _____ and _____ the same/different? Why? What/Who does this action remind you of? Why?
Reflection and Recall Questions	How did you like the character/plot/information? Would you say that the character is _____? Why? What did you learn from . . . ? What was this story about? What do we know about____?

FIGURE 8.3. Questions to ask for each strategy.

text and knowledge they already have to form an estimated guess on the content of what will follow in their reading. Prediction supports students in paying attention to the content and activating relevant knowledge that can assist in the meaning-making process. Asking predicting questions can occur before, during, and after reading.

Before reading, a good goal is to activate students' knowledge so they will consider how ideas that they already know connect with ideas in the text. To do so, you can ask questions that relate to the title or pictures on the cover. Using what they know from prior knowledge and clues from the title or pictures, students can make intelligent "guesses" about what the book may be about. Even if we use the term *guess*, students should be encouraged to make good guesses based on clues. You can guide students in making good guesses that fit with clues from the picture or the title.

During reading, you can stop and ask questions to monitor students' evolving understanding. These questions may connect with the students' previous prediction (Was it correct? Why?) and the formation of a new prediction in light of new information (Using what you learned so far and what you know, what do you think will happen next?). The students will need to once again use the clues from what was read and what they know about the specific information to "guess" what will follow or how the story will end.

Finally, after reading the book, your questions can prompt students to consider what they have already learned about the character or the events and predict on the basis of the information they heard and their own knowledge what might happen in the future. For example, after reading the book *If You Take a Mouse to School* by

Laura Numeroff (2002), you may ask students what the mouse will ask for next. The students will respond according to their understanding of events they have already heard in the text.

Something that we would like to caution you about is the need to ask for explanations of a prediction. It is a good idea to ask students to explain why they made the prediction they did. This explanation will give you even more insight into students' thinking and will support you in evaluating whether they have used strategic processes or wild guesses to make their predictions. For example, when asking children to predict what they think will happen next in a story, a good follow-up question is "Why do you think that?" Asking students to explain their prediction requires them to articulate their thinking process. Making comprehension visible is an important tool for correcting misunderstandings in students' thinking and for modeling for other students how and why a student came to the conclusion he or she did.

Open-ended questions are a type of question that relies on "How?" and "Why?" (Hargrave & Senechal, 2000; Wasik & Bond, 2001; Wasik et al., 2006; Whitehurst et al., 1994). These types of questions require students to evaluate the text's content and support the development of higher-order thinking. We find that these types of questions are more challenging for students, as they need to connect pieces of information and usually infer something that the author may not have mentioned. These "I wonder why" questions do not ask for information that is present in the text, but set a challenging task. This task can include taking the perspective of the character or viewing the events from a specific point of view. Good "Why?" questions ask students to think and feel as the character, to put him- or herself in the situation described and to use information presented in the text to provide an accurate response. Determining when to ask the "Why?" and "How?" questions can take a little time to plan; however, the benefit to students of including them throughout a read-aloud is far greater.

Teaching students to make *text-to-self connections* and *text-to-text connections* are additional skills that you can develop in your read-alouds. Although both require connections, the types of connections are quite different. In text-to-self connections, students use information they read to think of occasions when the characters' emotions or actions resembled their own (Justice et al., 2002; Morrow, 2001; Neuman & Celano, 2001; Wasik et al., 2006). In order to make text-to-self connections, students must consider specific information described in the text and locate in their experiences an equivalent situation. When you are preparing your questions for text-to-self connections, choose memorable events or emotions in the story to which you think many of your students can relate. A good text-to-self connection is based on universal emotions or experiences that everyone has experienced at some point in his or her life. For example, feeling sad is an emotion that every student listening to the read-aloud can relate to in some way.

Text-to-text connections ask students to form a connective bridge between what they have heard through your reading and another book that you have read (Bus,

2001; McGee & Schickedanz, 2007; Morrow, 1987, 2004; Paris & Paris, 2003; Pressley, 2000). This procedure requires that students will have background knowledge about a different book they have read and can make a connection between the two books. For this skill to be developed at least two sources need to have a common characteristic. For example, students can make a connection between a book with a character who is attending a party with a different book the class read with a character also attending a party. Once again, the best way to develop the skill is not only to ask students to make the connection but to be able to explain it in as much detail as possible. It will not be enough for the students to say, "This book reminds me of that book," but to also explain if the connection was made on the level of the character, the plot, the characters' actions or emotions, or events or topics. In our previous example, students could discuss the two different parties in the books read, comparing and contrasting what was similar and what was different. On some occasions you may read nonfiction texts on the same topic so the students will develop their knowledge. In that case the connections will be on the topic but the students can also explain what they have already learned from the previous book.

A final type of question you can ask young students during read-alouds are *reflection* or *recall questions*. These questions ask students to reflect on what was read (Wasik & Bond, 2001; Wasik et al., 2006). This reflection can take the form of a summary or evaluation of the information and the events (Morrow, 2001; Neuman, 1999; Neuman & Celano, 2001). Students use the information they heard and their judgment to form an opinion on the overall text and explain the reasons for their beliefs. In addition, they may provide specific information on events that took place. Again, you should always ask for an explanation of the students' responses.

We have provided a selection of strategies you can use for the development of comprehension. Figure 8.4 is a quick reference list of those strategies. We anticipate that it will work as a reminder of what should be included in your read-aloud time and how to ask meaningful questions that will promote thinking and discussion.

Prediction Questions	Provide questions that allow children to predict what a story may be about, what might happen next, or how the story might end.
Open-Ended Questions	Provide questions that include use of "Why?" "How?" or other open-ended questions through the majority of the reading.
Text-to-Self Connection Questions	Provide questions that allow children to make text-to-self connections to characters, setting, or story events.
Text-to-Text Connection Questions	Provide questions that allow children to make connections to other texts that they have read.
Reflection and Recall Questions	Provide questions at the end of the story that allow children to reflect, summarize, or connect to the story just read.

FIGURE 8.4. Best practices in comprehension instruction.

Planning Template

To help you plan a comprehension-focused read-aloud, we provide you with a planning template in Figure 8.5. The template addresses the specific strategies and skills necessary for comprehension development. These are (1) prediction questions, (2) open-ended questions, (3) self-to-text connection questions, (4) text-to-text connection questions, and (5) reflection and recall questions. The purpose of the template is to guide you in the types of questions you can ask while reading aloud. Our goal is to support you while planning and reflecting on your individualized read-alouds with students. A blank version of the template is available in the Appendix (Form 6).

To support you in the use of the template, consider the example of a first-grade teacher. Mr. Lee is a first-grade teacher at Argos Elementary School. He has taught first grade for 7 years, and he is considered to be a caring teacher among his colleagues. Mr. Lee has a classroom of 14 boys and 13 girls. Twenty of the students attended Argos Elementary the previous year and 7 are from different kindergarten classrooms in the district. Out of the 27 students, 6 are second-language learners, and 3 have an IEP for specific academic difficulties. Based on the weekly tests and end-of-unit assessments Mr. Lee recognizes the need for supporting his students' comprehension development and strengthening their application of specific skills.

Even if students' decoding skills is one of the prioritized goals of first grade, Mr. Lee acknowledges the need for the development of listening comprehension. Mr. Lee is aware that through listening comprehension he can make the application of strategic processes for meaning making visible to his students and support them in the development of necessary skills that they will be able to apply once they can read independently. Therefore, he wants to support his students in applying strategies for meaning making once they are able to read books on their own. Mr. Lee has devoted time in his everyday instruction for a read-aloud. This is part of the everyday routine, and the students as well as Mr. Lee always look forward to the read-aloud time. The selection of books that Mr. Lee reads are either based on the unit and theme they examine in his language arts core program, on seasonal themes, or on issues they discuss across the curriculum in social studies or science.

Mr. Lee has decided to read the book *One Fine Day* by Nonny Hogrogian (1971) during his morning read-aloud. He selected this book because it has a sequential structure and provides an excellent opportunity for questions on cause and effect. This book is a Caldecott Award book (*www.ala.org*), and its content and structure provide plenty of instructional opportunities to incorporate in his teaching. The story is about a fox that attempts to drink milk from an old woman's container and ends up losing its tail, which becomes the old woman's possession. The fox needs to bring something to the old woman to get its tail back. However, when he tries to get what she needs, he has to bring something else to the next person. The story lends itself to cause-and-effect sequences and to rich discussions, and Mr. Lee is positive that his students will enjoy it as much as he does every time he reads it.

A Focus on Comprehension Development in Read-Alouds

	Planning What is my plan?	Reflecting How did I do?	Goal Setting What will I do next time?
Prediction Questions	• What do you think this book will be about? Why? • What do you think the old woman would do once she sees that the fox drank her milk? • Was the initial prediction correct? Why? What will happen next? • Now that the fox went to the field what do you think will happen? Why? • Now that the fox finally got the grain what do you think she will do?		
Open-Ended Questions	• Why did the old woman chop off the fox's tail? • Do you think that what the fox did was respectful? Why? • Why did the cow ask for grass? • How do you think the fox feels? Why?		
Text-to-Self Connection Questions	• Have you ever done something that was not acceptable and you had some consequences? • Did you feel like the fox? How?		
Text-to-Text Connection Questions	• Do you remember when we read *Strega Nona*? Are there any similarities between that book and this one? (Do you think that the fox and Anthony have any similarities?)		
Reflection and Recall Questions	• What did the maiden ask from the fox? Why?		

FIGURE 8.5. Mr. Lee's initial planning template.

Using the planning template, Mr. Lee recorded the questions he wanted to ask before, during, and after reading. Figure 8.5 contains Mr. Lee's planning prior to the reading. Mr. Lee knows that predicting and repredicting is an essential strategy for monitoring the unfolding of a plot in a story. Therefore, he has made a plan to model for his students the application of the prediction strategy and guide them in the use of clues to form a prediction, examine its correctness, and repredict when necessary. While planning he carefully reread the book and placed "sticky notes" on pages that would remind him when to ask his questions. He knew that this was a good technique that saved time in the process of instruction.

In addition, Mr. Lee planned to ask his students open-ended questions that would bring to the surface the cause and effects of the fox's actions and the other characters' actions and reactions. These "Why?" and "How?" questions that Mr. Lee had in mind and recorded on his notes were meant to support students as they used critical thinking skills.

Mr. Lee also planned to use the well-structured plot and ask retelling questions. With his students he was working on retelling procedures using the beginning, middle, and end format of fiction texts, and *One Fine Day* (Hogrogian, 1971) was an excellent book to review retelling. Further, the well- structured plot could support the use of recall questions as the actions of the fox and the other characters were in a sequence and would assist in the recall of specific actions. In the following section, we follow Mr. Lee as he implements the read-aloud and applies the questioning strategies he had planned.

Implementing the Reading

Mr. Lee is well aware that his students will not be able to apply comprehension strategies successfully without his support. Further, he considers his students' responses as opportunities to explore their understanding and to think aloud when needed to make the thinking processes visible. Having completed the planning template for the book *One Fine Day* (Hogrogian, 1971), Mr. Lee is ready for his read-aloud. In the following section we hear some of his sample talk during the read-aloud.

Teacher Talk during Read-Alouds

Mr. Lee asks one of his students to read the class schedule to see what the next part of their day will be. Suzan reads from the posted schedule, "*Read-aloud,*" and Mr. Lee explains to his students that today they will read a book called *One Fine Day* by Nonny Hogrogian (1971). Mr. Lee says, "*You have been doing an excellent job listening carefully to our readings and applying your strategies to respond to questions. We will read this new book. As we read, we will discuss what the author tells us about the characters and their actions.*" As he shows the book, the students identify the Caldecott medal. Mr. Lee explains that the book has received an award for its artwork.

Mr. Lee reads the title and shows the cover picture to the students saying, *"The title is* **One Fine Day.** *On the cover, I see a picture of a fox. Looking at the picture and the title what do you think this book will be about?"* Many students raise their hands, and Mr. Lee asks them to turn to their partner and share their prediction and their thinking that lead them to it.

Once the students have shared their ideas with a partner, Mr. Lee asks Lakeisha to share her prediction. Lakeisha says, *"I think it is about a fox."*

"Why do you think that, Lakeisha?" asks Mr. Lee.

"Because I see a fox on the cover."

Mr. Lee points to the prediction poster he had created and says, *"So, do you think that the book will be about a fox's fine day? Remember the title of the book is* **One Fine Day.** *Keeping the title of the book in your mind, looking at the picture, and thinking of what a fine day might look like, what would you predict?"*

Lakeisha says, *"It is about a fox that was at the forest and played with other animals."*

"That is a great prediction, Lakeisha. How did you come up with the idea that the fox was going to play with other animals?" asks Mr. Lee.

Lakeisha pauses and says, *"Because when I have a good day I play with my friend at my friend's house."*

Mr. Lee congratulates Lakeisha for using what she knew about the title and the picture to make a good prediction. He says, *"So, Lakeisha thought of the title that was about a fine day, how the fox would have a great day, and the picture on the cover that showed a fox to make a prediction that the book would be about a fox that had a fine day in the forest playing with other animals. Do you think her prediction is a good one? Thumbs up if you think it is good, middle if it could be better, or down if you think it is not complete."* The students put their thumbs up, and Mr. Lee writes the prediction on the board.

After reading the second page of the book he asks, *"What do you think the old woman will do once she sees that the fox drank her milk? What do you think, Yiota?"*

Yiota looks at Mr. Lee and says with a smile, *"She will get angry."*

"Why do you think that?" asks Mr. Lee.

"Because that is her milk," says Yiota.

Mr. Lee turns to Christian, who is fidgeting in his chair, and asks, *"What do you think, Christian?"*

Christian turns to Mr. Lee and says, *"I think she will chase her and the fox will run away."*

Mr. Lee reads the next page and asks, *"Do you think that our prediction about the reaction of the old lady was correct or not? One finger up if you think yes, two up if you were wrong. Wow! Most of you thought it was correct. Why do you think that, Tariya?"*

"*The old lady got angry and cut the fox's tail. She didn't like it that the fox drank her milk and said, 'Give me back my milk!'*" says Tariya.

"*That is correct,*" says Mr. Lee. "*The old woman got very angry and she physically hurt the fox. Do you think that the prediction we made at the beginning of our book was correct or not?*" The students raise one finger up. "*Why do you think it was incorrect, Lakeisha?*"

"*Because the fox is hurt and is not playing with the animals.*"

"*That is a very good prediction,*" says Mr. Lee.

"*I think that the fox has done something that was not acceptable by the old lady and as a result she has to now face the consequence of her action. For example, once I spoke back to my sister and I insulted her in front of her friends. My sister was upset with me and she didn't want to take me ever again with her. Have you ever done something that was unacceptable and you had to face a consequence? What would you like to share with us, Marco?*"

"*One day I took all my toys out of my toy basket and after I played I did not put them away. My mom was upset and she said that I would have no toys for a whole day!*" says Marco.

"*Thank you for sharing with us, Marco. So the consequence for you was not playing with your toys for a whole day. How did you feel then?*"

"*I didn't like it . . . and I was bored. I was mad, too, but my mom said we have to learn from our mistakes,*" Marco says with a sincere voice.

"*Do you think that you and fox shared the same feelings?*" asks Mr. Lee. After seeing Marco nodding positively he continues by asking, "*What are those feelings?*"

"*I was sad and the fox is sad. I was mad, too, and maybe the fox is mad and says inside her head, 'Why did I drink that milk?'*" Marco adds with animations.

"*That is very possible, Marco! Let's continue. As you were listening to this story, did you think of another story we read about someone who also did something that he was not supposed to do? I will be more specific. Remember when we read the book **Strega Nona** by Tomie dePaola? Can you think of any similarities between that book and this one? What do you think, Taria?*" asks Mr. Lee.

"*Anthony did not listen,*" says Taria with a loud and clear voice.

"*What do you mean? Help us understand better,*" adds Mr. Lee.

"*Anthony tried to do magic things when Strega Nona was not there and there was a mess of spaghetti everywhere!*" says Taria and opens her arms as she explains.

"*Is there a similarity with the fox you think?*" asks Mr. Lee.

"*Well, no one told the fox not to have milk . . . but . . . it was not her milk, and she shouldn't have drunk it. And Anthony shouldn't have tried to do magic! Strega Nona was not there and she knew the magic!*" continues Taria.

"*I think that Taria found a great similarity between those two characters. Don't you think?*" asks Mr. Lee. The students agree and remembering what happened to Anthony with the spaghetti start laughing.

"*Friends, what do you predict will happen next? Earlier Lakeisha told us about our first prediction. Lakeisha, would you like to share what you think would happen next?*" asks Mr. Lee.

Lakeisha thinks for a while and after looking back at the pictures of the book says, "*The fox will have to go get some milk for the old woman.*"

"*Where do you think the fox will go?*" asks Mr. Lee.

"*It may go to a cow or in the supermarket,*" says Lakeisha.

Mr. Lee smiles, congratulates his student for using her knowledge to make a prediction, and turns to Maria to ask, "*Do you think that what the fox did was respectful? What do you think, Maria?*"

"*No, it was not,*" says Maria.

"*I agree with you, Maria,*" says Mr. Lee, who turns to Reid and asks him, "*Why was it not respectful, Reid?*"

Reid says, "*Because the old woman needed that milk and the fox didn't ask if she could have it, and it was the same as stealing because the old woman was not looking.*"

Reid's response is given almost in one breath, and Mr. Lee repeats it by restating the initial question. He turns to Reid and says, "*That is a nice response, Reid. I liked that you used evidence from the story, and you concluded that the fox was stealing.*" Mr. Lee continues, "*Remember in your responses to restate the question, answer, and support what you believe using text information.*"

Mr. Lee reads the next page and asks, "*Why did the cow ask for grass? Patrick?*"

Patrick raises his hand and with excitement responds, "*She asked for grass because she eats vegetables and she can make milk if she is well fed, so she needs more grass.*"

"*That is a good reason, Patrick,*" says Mr. Lee. He looks around at the class and asks, "*Anyone else? Kathryn?*"

"*I think that the fox needs to pay the cow and she pays it with grass,*" Kathryn responds.

"*That would be another reason. Great response, Kathryn! When we buy something, we have to pay for it. So, since the fox needs something from the cow, she needs to pay the cow or perhaps trade with the cow: I will give you milk, you will give me grass,*" explains Mr. Lee, elaborating on Kathryn's response.

Mr. Lee proceeds with his reading. In the next few pages of the book he asks the students to check the new content and compare it to their initial predictions. He also asks them questions that require the students to make inferences and use the information heard and their world knowledge to make a cohesive response.

A few pages later he asks, "*Now that the fox finally got the grain, what will she do? Taria, would you like to answer this question?*"

Taria looks up from her desk and says, "*She will give it to the hen, and then the hen will give her the egg, and she will give it to the peddler to get the bread, and he will give the bread to the girl, and she will give him the jug, and he will get the water and give it to the field, and the field will give grass to give to the cow, and the cow will give her milk to give to the lady to give her her tail."*

Mr. Lee claps with enthusiasm to Taria's response and comments, *"Wow! Taria, that was a very good sequence of all the events we just read, but going backward."* Mr. Lee reads the next few pages, *"What do you think the fox will do now that its tail is back in place? Marsha?"*

Marsha responds, *"It will go on its walk."*

"Yes," says Mr. Lee, *"I also think that now that the fox has its tail it will go on its walk. That sounds like a good way to finish her day, and perhaps as Lakeisha had said at the beginning she will play with her friends."*

After completing the book, Mr. Lee asks several recall questions: *"What did the fox ask from the maiden and why? Lia, would you like to share your thoughts?"*

"It asked for the jug to bring the water to the field," says Lia.

"That is correct," says Mr. Lee, elaborating on Lia's response, *"since the field needed the water and fox could not carry the water from the stream she needed a jug."* Then Mr. Lee asks an evaluation question that refers to the initial title of the book: *"Do you think that the fox had a fine day, and why? Peter, what do you think?"*

Peter pauses for a while trying to make up his mind and responds, *"I think that at the beginning she had a horrible day, but her day was fine again."*

Mr. Lee agrees with Peter and explains his reasoning, *"I think the same thing, too. At the beginning once she lost her tail she must have had a horrible day, especially since she had to walk from one place to another asking for different items. In the end, though, her day returned to normal and it was fine again."* Mr. Lee concludes, *"Today we read the book **One Fine Day** by Nonny Hogrogian, and we were very good readers and listeners as we predicted using clues, thought carefully about the feelings of the fox, and discussed her actions."*

Reflecting on the Reading

During his planning period, Mr. Lee returned to the planning template to record his reflections on the success of his read-aloud. He prefers to complete his reflections a few hours after the read-aloud so he can still recall his students' responses. Mr. Lee used the time that his students were in music class to revisit his plans and compare the lesson with them. Mr. Lee's completed template is presented in Figure 8.6.

Thinking about Strengths and Challenges

Mr. Lee enjoyed reading the book with his students, and he was delighted to see their engagement. The selection of the book was an appropriate and a successful one as the students enjoyed listening to the fox's adventure and responding to questions that required them to think deeply about the fox and the characters' emotions and

A Focus on Comprehension Development in Read-Alouds

	Planning What is my plan?	Reflecting How did I do?	Goal Setting What will I do next time?
Prediction Questions	• What do you think this book will be about? Why? • What do you think the old woman would do once she sees that the fox drank her milk? • Was the initial prediction correct? Why? What will happen next? • Now that the fox went to the field what do you think will happen? Why? • Now that the fox finally got the grain what do you think she will do?	• Students shared their first predictions with a partner but did not do so again. • I supported Lakeisha but not Yiota. • Prediction was not easy for Lakeisha and not all students participated. • I did not include prediction on my questions during the rest of the book, but only at rare occasions.	• Allow students to share their responses with a partner. • Follow the same format of responses and prompting with all students. • Provide additional think-alouds on how to form a prediction using clues and give opportunity to students to make their own prediction by stating the clues used. • Work on prediction throughout the book and not only at the beginning.
Open-Ended Questions	• Why did the old woman chop off the fox's tail? • Do you think that what the fox did was respectful? Why? • Why did the cow ask for grass? • How do you think the fox feels? Why?	• I gave no time for Maria to support her answer. I did not prompt her to support her response. • I did not prompt Peter to give me a complete response. I did not give time for the students to share their thinking.	• Allow students to share responses with a partner. • Ask the students to explain the reasons for their responses.
Text-to-Self Connection Questions	• Have you ever done something that was not acceptable and you had some consequences? • Did you feel like the fox? How?	• I asked Marco to share, but I did not give the opportunity for sharing to any other student.	• Give opportunities to other students to make connections between the book and their experiences.
Text-to-Text Connection Questions	• Do you remember when we read *Strega Nona*? Are there any similarities between that book and this one? (Do you think that the fox and Anthony have any similarities?)	• I asked Taria and she analyzed how the characters were similar, but she also pointed out the differences in the conditions.	• Consider using books of themes that allow such connections. The students would be able to better understand the characters and make inferences about their feelings and situations.
Reflection and Recall Questions	• What did the maiden ask from the fox? Why?	• I did not ask Peter for an elaboration on his response and support using text evidence. • I asked only one recall question.	• Allow students to share responses with a partner. • Prompt the students to use complete responses and provide evidence to support them. • Provide students with time to retell and review the content of the book.

FIGURE 8.6. Mr. Lee's completed template.

intentions. Also, he found that giving time to the students to talk with a classmate prior to responding gave the opportunity for all students to develop an idea and share it with a friend. Even when he found the students' engagement encouraging, he identified areas where he could have further supported their learning.

At the beginning of the read-aloud Mr. Lee asked the students to share with a partner their prediction of what the book might be about. This was something he did not do in any other part of his read-aloud. Mr. Lee thinks that it might be a good idea to ask students to share their responses with a partner more often throughout the read-aloud, and he sets this as a goal for his next reading with his students.

When working with connections, Mr. Lee was pleased to see how engaged Marco was to share his personal experience and connect it with the character in the book. However, Mr. Lee realized that he did not give the same opportunity to other students. He decides this strategy could be a powerful aid to students' comprehension and makes a plan to ask more students to make text-to-self connections in future read-alouds. Also, when he asked the question about the similarities between the fox and Anthony, he realized that Taria was able to analyze her thinking and not only identify the similarity between the two characters but also the difference in the conditions of disobedience. Mr. Lee made a plan to continue developing students' text-to-text connections in future read-alouds.

At the beginning stage of his instruction, once Lakeisha provided an incomplete prediction, Mr. Lee supported her by revisiting the clues and prompting her background knowledge in order to form an accurate prediction. However, he did not follow the same prompting when Yiota provided a short repetitive response. On the contrary, he proceeded with Christian. Mr. Lee set his goal to always make the thinking process visible to all his students without exception. In regard to prediction, he also noticed that Lakeisha had difficulty retrieving the clues and noticed that not all students used all the clues in their explanations to their partners. Since prediction is a very useful strategy, Mr. Lee sets a goal to provide additional think-alouds and opportunities to his students to form predictions and explain their own thinking. Further, Mr. Lee noticed that since the book structure could work effectively with forming additional predictions, he did not continue the application of the strategy through questioning. Mr. Lee commented on the reflection column and set a goal of working on prediction throughout the book and not only at its beginning.

When Mr. Lee asked open-ended and evaluation questions, he was pleased to see that most of the students provided their opinion. However, their responses were not always supported. For example, when Peter was asked whether the fox's day was fine, he did respond, but his response was not supported. Mr. Lee realized that instead of asking for Peter to use the evidence from the text it was he who elaborated on Peter's reasoning, without prompting Peter or reminding him to use text evidence to support his opinion. Perhaps Peter would have supported his opinion if Mr. Lee had waited for his response or asked for it. Mr. Lee could not tell whether Peter was not able to use explanation or whether he did not know the answer. Therefore, he set as his goal to always ask his students to support their reasoning. Also, Mr. Lee asked Maria for her response and she responded with a yes/no answer. Mr. Lee did not wait for her to respond, but asked Reid whose answer began with "because." Perhaps Maria would have been able to provide additional support to her response if Mr. Lee had asked her.

Finally, after reading, Mr. Lee limited himself to one recall question. He should have asked questions that revisited the structure of the text instead of rushing through; however, he simply ran out of time. Perhaps he could have asked the students to retell the book with a partner. By doing so all his students would have been able to remember the content of the book and then respond to his questions without taking a long time to retrieve the information from memory. Mr. Lee's goal during his next read-aloud is to ask additional recall questions and give time to the students to retell the book to a partner. He also sets a goal of researching graphic organizers and story maps that may help him record students' retelling responses visually on the board.

Closing Thoughts

Comprehension is a critical component of reading and reading instruction. Through your read-alouds you have the opportunity to model problem-solving strategies and also engage your students in thoughtful discussions through questioning. These questioning approaches include (1) prediction questions, (2) open-ended questions, (3) self-to-text connection questions, (4) text-to-text connection questions, and (5) reflection and recall questions. Your questions can ask students to make predictions, inferences, connections between self and text or text and text, and summary statements. We encourage you to use the provided template (Figure 8.5) to help plan, reflect on, and set goals for read-alouds to develop students' comprehension. A blank planning template for developing comprehension is located in the Appendix.

CHAPTER 9

Tracking Your Progress

So far we have approached each key literacy component in isolation, considering how you might develop children's phonological awareness or vocabulary or comprehension during read-alouds. Especially when you are just beginning to plan your read-alouds or when you are working with very young children new to the classroom environment, you may want to plan read-alouds that focus on one discrete skill. However, we know that in order to maximize the instructional potential of each read-aloud to develop the skills absolutely necessary in preparing young children for literacy, it makes more sense to plan read-alouds that target combinations of skills.

In this chapter we consider how to prepare thoughtful combinations of literacy skills in the same read-aloud. First, we take a look at important considerations when preparing skill combinations. Then we revisit three classroom teachers to see how each approaches the task of planning read-alouds that develop multiple literacy skills. We hope that our teachers' examples will give you insight into their planning process. Finally, we conclude with some final thoughts about the read-aloud experience in preschool and primary grades.

Important Considerations

When thinking about which literacy skills make the most sense to combine in one read-aloud, several considerations can help inform your planning process. We recommend thinking about three primary criteria: grade-level demands, student needs, and book characteristics.

Grade-Level Demands

Certainly your school's grade-level demands and state or national Common Core State Standards (CCSS) will help shape the skills addressed by your instruction. The national CCSS address the key literacy skills we have included in this text: oral language, vocabulary, print conventions, phonological awareness, and comprehension. Indeed, these areas of literacy development are pretty typical across individual state and national standards, because they are the essential building blocks of preparing young children for reading. For example, the national CCSS in the area of Print Concepts for kindergarten suggest that in kindergarten students should be able to demonstrate competence in directionality, relationship of letters and sounds, spacing, and alphabet. In grade 1, students should be able to develop understanding and competence on the organization of print and function of print features.

These literacy goals, as described by the national CCSS, are addressed in the planning template we propose and will assist you in better addressing these goals for your grade level. Knowledge of your grade's standards and also the preceding grade-level demands and those of the subsequent grade level will help you situate your students along a continuum of learning and help to inform your instruction. If you know the literacy skills students coming into your class have and those skills they will build upon in the next grade level, you will be better able to meet the needs of your children while they are with you.

Student Needs

In addition to grade-level demands, knowledge of student needs will most certainly inform how you decide what literacy skills to develop during read-alouds. Only you and the professionals working with you know the unique literacy needs of each child. The assessment measures you use—perhaps a concepts-of-print inventory or a phonological awareness skills subtest—will give you with information about which student needs support developing which literacy skill or skills. For example, you may know from an alphabet knowledge measure that several students in your class can identify all the letters in the alphabet but are struggling with letter sounds, whereas a phonological awareness measure may have alerted you to several students who are really struggling with rhyme. This valuable information from assessments can help inform your planning of a read-aloud to target both alphabet knowledge and phonological awareness to meet your students' needs.

Book Characteristics

Last, as we have discussed in each chapter, certain books lend themselves to the development of some literacy skills over others. For example, an alphabet book by its very subject and content makes it ideal for targeting students' alphabet knowledge.

A picture book with rich character development, a unique setting, and an interesting plot may be perfect for engaging students in conversation to develop their oral language, vocabulary, and comprehension simultaneously. A close examination of the text you will be reading to children prior to the actual read-aloud can help determine its characteristics and how best to use those characteristics to your advantage to build children's emergent literacy.

As you plan for combinations of literacy skills in a single read-aloud, consideration of your grade-level demands, the unique literacy needs of your students, and the characteristics of your classroom books will help you to maximize your instructional impact and offer the most support to your students' literacy development. Figure 9.1 summarizes the important considerations to keep in mind when making decisions about literacy combinations in a single read-aloud.

Revisiting Our Teachers' Classrooms

In each chapter of this book, we have discussed the benefits of planning and reflecting on developing individual literacy skills in read-alouds. In addition, we described the instructional benefits of combining skills during your read-aloud time. In the following section we provide examples of combined skills practices for each one of the grade levels that have been introduced in previous chapters. We will revisit the classrooms of Mrs. French in PreK, Mrs. Tragas in kindergarten, and Mr. Lee in first grade in order to see how they determined what skills to combine in a single read-aloud experience. The combinations the teachers in our case studies used are only examples that are unique to each teacher's grade-level demands, the needs of the students in their classrooms, and the types of books the teachers chose to work with. Remember that you can combine a variety of skills. You only need to keep in mind your grade-level instructional goals, your students' needs, and potential skills the book you selected address. Keeping these considerations in mind, let's revisit the classrooms of our teachers.

Grade-Level Demands	• What literacy skills are addressed by the standards your school uses, either state or national CCSS? • What literacy understandings do your students come to you with from earlier stages of reading development? What literacy understandings do your students need to know to be successful at the next grade level?
Student Needs	• Based on assessment measures, what literacy skills have individual students mastered? What literacy skills do individual students need to further refine and develop? • How can your read-aloud meet the range of literacy needs of your students?
Book Characteristics	• What makes this book special? • Which literacy skills jump off the page ripe for discussion?

FIGURE 9.1. Considerations for combining literacy skills in a read-aloud.

PreK: Mrs. French

Remember Mrs. French from Chapter 3? Mrs. French is a prekindergarten teacher and we have seen her planning and reflecting while working on oral language development. Mrs. French has been monitoring her students' classroom engagement and oral language use, and she is excited to see that her students are able to raise questions on the content of books they read, share experiences that connect with the content of the book, and participate in shared discussions. Mrs. French, though, is aware that for her preschoolers to be successful in their first year of kindergarten she needs to also address skills that connect to the students' book and print awareness as well as develop an understanding of the alphabet and its function in print. In making her decision on what to plan for, Mrs. French consults the content of her grade-level standards and discusses with her grade-level colleagues their next instructional goals. Mrs. French knows from her informal observations that some of her students are able to name the letters in their names; however, they are not able to correctly identify additional letters. Further, some of her students are able to distinguish between words and pictures, and she has observed that when they "pretend read" they move their fingers from left to right on the page. However, instead of return sweep when they get to the end of a line, her students tend to move their finger from right to left. Therefore, Mrs. French sets a goal of combining the skills of print awareness and alphabet recognition in her very next read-aloud. She is aware that she will need to provide additional instruction to support the effective application of those skills, and she intends to plan for those additional opportunities during her instruction throughout the classroom day.

When selecting a book to use, Mrs. French looks for a big book that will allow all students to easily see the print and illustrations. In addition, following the criteria of a book selection, she looks for a book with clear, realistic pictures and print that presents the letters clearly, without added detail. Mrs. French chooses to use *The Farm Alphabet Book*, a nonfiction text, by Jane Miller (2000). This book has a clear but engaging front cover, and each page inside connects an upper-case and lower-case letter with a word and information related to a picture beginning with the letter sound. Its content also connects to the unit she is currently working on with students about farm animals and Mrs. French knows that it has the potential to also be used for oral language development and reading comprehension in future read-alouds.

Prior to using the book with her students, Mrs. French makes a change on the lower-case letter *a* to resemble the lowercase *a* the students would see in the cards she has displayed in her classroom. She plans to introduce this graphic representation of the letter in a follow-up lesson. When drafting her plan for the read-aloud, Mrs. French reviews the best practices for the development of print awareness (you may find those in Chapter 5) and the best practices for the development of alphabet knowledge (you may find those in Chapter 6). Mrs. French's planning can be seen completed in Figure 9.2.

Mrs. French has completed the planning of her lesson. As you may have noticed, we did not include the reflection and goal-setting section of the template because our goal was to illustrate the practice and thinking process she followed when planning

	Planning: What is my plan?
Front of Book	I will point to the front cover and explain the function of the front cover in "attracting" and informing the reader of the book's content. I will ask students to point to the front cover.
Back of Book	I will ask the students to show the back cover of the book. We will discuss the function of the back cover.
Title of Book	I will point to the title, read it, and ask the students to discuss what the use of the title is. Then I will ask more than one student to point to the title and "read it."
Role of Author	I will name the author and ask the students to explain his or her role. We have discussed this strategy in other books and my students should be able to explain the author's role.
Role of Illustrator and Photographer	The photographer and the author is the same person in this text. I will ask the students to discuss what the "photographer" contributes to a book and what other roles the author of this book has besides having written the words.
Top-to-Bottom Progression	When beginning to read information about each picture, I will point and count the number of lines of print. I will ask more than one student to repeat after me. I will also explain why we read from top to bottom.
Left-to-Right Progression	I will track print and ask a student to track print after me. I will move my finger from one word to the next and show the students how to track. I will ask more than one student to repeat after me.
Return Sweep	I will model return sweep. I will ask more than one student to repeat after me. Then, I will ask students to direct me to the next line as I read.
Identify Any Letter	I will ask students to identify any letters on the cover. I will do the same when opening to the title page.
Identify Specific Letter/Letters	I will focus on the letters *B* and *R*. Whenever I come across either letter in the text, I will point it out to the students and ask them to identify it after me. Then I will call students to identify these letters.
Identify a Letter in Child's Own Name	After every two or three pages, I will invite the students to search the text to find letters in their own names.
Sound–Symbol Correspondence	I will model the sound the letters *B* and *R* make. I will say the letter name and sound and ask for more than one student to repeat after me. I will do that throughout the text.

FIGURE 9.2. Mrs. French's planning template: Print awareness and alphabet recognition.

for the combination of those targeted skills. However, after implementation, Mrs. French would participate in the same reflection process she engaged in when implementing her read-aloud focused on oral language exclusively in Chapter 3.

Kindergarten: Mrs. Tragas

Remember Mrs. Tragas from Chapter 5? In that chapter we saw her as she applied our template to develop print conventions and book awareness. Mrs. Tragas is a kindergarten teacher who has proudly observed her students' growth during the school year. She faced challenges in her instruction because many of her students had attended preschool and lacked important school-readiness skills. However, through her systematic planning and reflecting, with ample opportunities to revisit texts, she has seen them grow, develop, and apply skills related to print conventions, alphabet knowledge, and comprehension.

Mrs. Tragas's school has developed a teacher-friendly binder of the state standards, and Mrs. Tragas carefully examines those skills her students have developed to mastery, those skills they are still developing, and the skills her students need additional support to understand. After consulting the standards and reviewing the data collected by the mid-year progress monitoring conducted by the school's reading specialist, Mrs. Tragas decides to work with her students on the combined skills of phonological awareness and oral language. Her goal is to support her students in responding to questions related to content, discussing information provided in the text, identifying and/or producing rhymes, and segmenting and blending syllables in words.

When deciding what book to use for this type of combined-skills read-aloud, Mrs. Tragas consulted the best practices for oral language development and phonological awareness from the previous chapters (Chapters 3 and 7, respectively). She decided to combine those skills because her students were in need of additional support in the development of skills related to rhyming and could further build their oral language skills with rich discussions. Mrs. Tragas looked carefully in her library for a book that had welcoming artwork, rich language, an engaging story line, and words that engaged the reader in a playful game with sounds. She selected the book *Pigs Aplenty, Pigs Galore!* by David McPhail (1996). This book with its playful application of rhyming, well-designed pictures, and clear story line allowed her to artfully combine phonological awareness and oral language instruction in the same read-aloud.

Mrs. Tragas drafted the planning of her instruction keeping in mind what her students were able to accomplish and what they still had to develop. Her planning template can be found in Figure 9.3.

Mrs. Tragas was pleased with her selection of the book to develop both oral language and phonological awareness. She used her planning template to plan a read-aloud with the goals of engaging her students in rich discussion and making them more conscious of the sounds in rhyming words. After implementing her read-aloud in the classroom, Mrs. Tragas would reflect on the successes of her students and set goals for future read-alouds.

Grade 1: Mr. Lee

Remember Mr. Lee, our first-grade teacher? We watched him thoughtfully plan his comprehension lesson in Chapter 8. Mr. Lee and his students are in the middle of the school year. So far he has modeled and supported his students in the application of comprehension strategies, and he is pleased with their performance on weekly comprehension skills assessments. His students are able to make predictions about

	Planning: What is my plan?
Rich Language Modeled	• I will discuss the information provided on the cover of the book. I will explain the meaning of the title and ask the students to discuss how the title connects with the pictures on the cover. I will describe the scene on the cover of the book in great detail and connect it to the title. • I will stop and discuss the actions of the character as he enters the kitchen and how what he sees connects with the reader's expectations as developed from the title of the book.
Open-Ended Questions	I will ask the following questions: • Why did the man leave his armchair and go to the kitchen? • Why are so many pigs in his kitchen? • Do you think that he is excited and pleased to pay the pizza bill? Why or why not? • Do you think it was nice for him to scream for the pigs to get out of his house? Why or why not? • What would you do if you were surrounded by so many hungry pigs?
Language Repetition and Expansion	I will repeat a student response and expand it by questioning or by adding information. Finally, I will repeat the complete response and call for students to repeat after me.
Language Follow-Up Prompts	If the students provide a "one-word" response, I will ask follow-up questions for them to elaborate.
Praise and Encouragement	Throughout our reading I will praise the students for using complete responses and for applying the language behaviors we are practicing.
Segmenting Syllables	• I will model how to break apart words into syllables by clapping them and ask for students to repeat the procedure with me. Some of the words we will work on are *reading, feeding, England, underpants,* and *doorbell.* • We will count the syllables and think about the compound word *underpants.*
Blending Syllables	After segmenting words into syllables, I will clap once and blend the syllables together to reconstruct the complete word. I will ask the students to assist me by repeating each word.
Rhyme Identification	I will read the first page of the book and ask the students if they hear "something musical" in the words. I will explain how the words rhyme, and I will ask them to listen for rhyming words in the book. After reading, I will provide pairs of words and ask them to identify the rhymes.
Rhyme Completion	After reading the repetitive phrases of the book, I will call on the students to attempt to compete the familiar phrase.
Rhyme Production	• As I read, I will leave the rhyme incomplete and ask the students to think of words that could complete the meaning of the sentence and rhyme with the previously provided word. For example, I will read, "I give them brooms, a pail, a mop. Now sweep and scrub till I say _____." • At the end of the reading, I will also ask the students to produce rhymes for the word *head.* We may attempt to develop a rhyme imitating the format of the book.

FIGURE 9.3. Mrs. Tragas's planning template: Phonological awareness and oral language.

the content of a book and to think about characters' actions; most students are able to retell the story line with his support and make connections between what they read and their own experiences.

However, Mr. Lee knows that comprehension can be inhibited by poor vocabulary, and he plans to add vocabulary instruction to his planning lessons. He knows that some of his students have opportunities to read outside of his classroom, and he can see how they apply the words they learn from additional readings to their conversations and writing. However, Mr. Lee is aware that this skill is one that all his students can improve for their general development as readers. Therefore, he considers combining the skills of vocabulary development and comprehension when planning his next read-aloud.

When deciding what book to select for his instruction, Mr. Lee thinks about the characteristics of books that support vocabulary development and comprehension (see Chapters 4 and 8, respectively). In addition, he reviews the best practices for supporting vocabulary development and instruction of Tier Two words before, during, and after reading (see Chapter 4, Figure 4.5). Mr. Lee selects the book *When I Was Young in the Mountains* by Cynthia Rylant (1982). This is a book of historical fiction, and he thinks that it will provide opportunities for his students to make connections and comparisons between the time narrated and the current time. It also has a clear story line and artwork that adds to and expands the meaning of the words. Mr. Lee completed his planning template taking into account the skills his students should develop by the end of the school year, his students' needs, and the instructional opportunities the specific book provides. His planning template can be found in Figure 9.4.

As he was planning his read-aloud, Mr. Lee recognized the great potential the book had for rich discussions and connections between students' lives and the text. He considered revisiting this text to further work on comprehension and review and expand the vocabulary words he could teach in future read-alouds. Mr. Lee acknowledged that he could not talk about everything the book offered to his students in a single read-aloud, making this book a good choice for repeated reading. In the next section, we further consider the benefits of repeated read-alouds of the same text to develop students' literacy skills.

Repeated Readings

As mentioned in Chapter 1, children love to have their favorite story read again and again. For children, it tends to elicit feelings of comfort and familiarity. For teachers, it represents multiple opportunities to develop key literacy and language skills in an authentic, engaging context. This idea of reading one text several times over the course of multiple days to children is called repeated readings. Repeated readings of books has been shown to increase children's language and vocabulary development (e.g., Wasik et al., 2006), comprehension of text (e.g., Neuman & Celano, 2001), and understandings of various genres and text structures (e.g., Paris & Paris, 2003).

	Planning: What is my plan?
Specific Word/s Introduction	I will introduce these words earlier as they may confuse the students. These are more Tier Three words than Tier Two. *Congregation*: when people who have the same religion and beliefs get together. *Baptism*: a procedure followed in specific religions when a person is put into water.
Specific Word/s Repeated (after reading)	I will ask the students to repeat the word after me when I introduce it and at the end after we provide a number of examples. My question will be "What is the word?"
Specific Word/s in Child-Friendly Terms (after reading)	After introducing and repeating the word, I will provide a child-friendly definition for each. *Covered*: *cover* means to place something over something with the purpose of protecting it. The word the author used is *covered*. *Promised*: to say that something will be done with the belief that you will do your best to do it.
Specific Word/s as Used in the Story (after reading)	I will write each word on the board. After writing each word I will reread the section of the text where the word was used. "Grandfather came home in the evening *covered* with the black dust of the coal mine." "I *promised* never to eat more than one serving of okra again." " . . . walked with the *congregation* through the cow pasture . . . " "to the dark swimming hole for *baptisms*"
Specific Word/s Used Outside the Story (after reading)	You may be *covered* in chocolate when you are eating ice cream. You may *cover* yourself with leaves to hide from your friends when you play hide and seek. I *promised* I will not lie to my older sister again. I *promise* I will teach you what you need to be ready for second grade. The *congregation* was loud and the priest asked everyone to be quiet. We all walked with the *congregation* to the study room. Angelo was crying loudly at his *baptism*. I cannot remember my *baptism* and how I was put into the water.
Specific Word/s Examples from Students	Ask children to give examples of the words: Were you ever *covered* by something? Have you ever made a *promise* to someone? Do you belong to a *congregation*? Have you ever been at a *baptism*?
Prediction Questions	What do you think this book will be about? Why? Where do you think the girl in this story lives? Why?
Open-Ended Questions	Why was the grandfather covered with coal? Why did the girl want her grandmother with her when she went to the bathroom? Why would she go outside? Why were they using a candle? Why did the children pump water from the well? Why did they heat the water for their baths? Why did the grandfather use his pocketknife to sharpen the girl's pencils?
Text-to-Self Connection Questions	Have you ever been to the mountains? What do you do in the middle of the night if you need to use the bathroom? In the baptisms you have seen, how are people baptized?
Reflection and Recall Questions	What did the children and their grandparents do at dinnertime? Why? What were some of the things that were taking place at the water hole? Why? Would you say that the children were scared of nature? Why? Would you say that life was easier back then? Why or why not?

FIGURE 9.4. Mr. Lee's planning template: Vocabulary and comprehension.

Consider the literacy and language targets that we have introduced in Chapters 3–8. Each of the literacy and language targets were introduced in isolation so that we could present the full range of strategies in each area of literacy and language that could be implemented in a read-aloud. Also, consider the information we have provided in this chapter about targeting multiple skills in one read-aloud. This being the case, it may be that you are targeting one area of instruction or you may be overlapping two areas in one read-aloud. For example, your focus may be oral language or oral language *and* vocabulary in one read-aloud session. Engaging in repeated readings provides you with the time to model these strategies and elicit participation from your students. It also provides students with enough opportunities to feel comfortable with and demonstrate their understanding of the strategies. In effect, planning for multiple, or repeated, readings of a book allows you to ensure student success.

Final Thoughts

In the previous chapters we provided specific approaches to plan and reflect on your instruction of essential reading components. The reflective approach we suggest is meant to support you in revising your lessons and in planning your future read-alouds. In this chapter we have also encouraged you to consider targeting more than one skill in a single read-aloud. It would be time-consuming to expect your students to reach mastery in any one of the skills before introducing another skill. By combining skills, you can work on developing several skills at the same time, maximizing the instructional potential of each and every read-aloud. Remember to consider the needs of your students, your grade-level goals, and the instructional opportunities of the book you are using when deciding which literacy skills to target. Finally, we encourage you to revisit the same book without hesitation. Repeated read-alouds offer many advantages to your instruction and to your students' growth as readers.

As an educator of young children, you are charged with the tremendous responsibility of shaping early literacy experiences to develop students' critical emergent literacy skills. Research indicates that read-alouds are the most effective context for developing students' literacy skills, including oral language, vocabulary, alphabet knowledge, phonological awareness, concepts of print, and comprehension. The good news is that read-alouds can be fun and rewarding for both you and your students. We hope that the suggestions we have included in this text help you as you begin to plan, implement, and reflect on the successes of your read-alouds. Happy reading!

Blank Planning Templates

FORM 1

A Focus on Oral Language Development in Read-Alouds

	Planning What is my plan?	Reflecting How did I do?	Goal Setting What will I do next time?
Rich Language Modeled			
Open-Ended Questions			
Language Repetition and Expansion			
Language Follow-Up Prompts			
Role of Listener			
Praise and Encouragement			

A Focus on Vocabulary in Read-Alouds

	Planning What is my plan?	Reflecting How did I do?	Goal Setting What will I do next time?
Vocabulary Introduction (before and after reading)			
Vocabulary Infused into Storybook (during reading)			
Vocabulary Repeated (after reading)			
Vocabulary in Child-Friendly Terms (after reading)			
Vocabulary Contextualized (after reading)			
Vocabulary in Other Contexts (after reading)			
Vocabulary Extended (after reading)			

A Focus on Book and Print Conventions in Read-Alouds

	Planning What is my plan?	Reflecting How did I do?	Goal Setting What will I do next time?
Front of Book			
Back of Book			
Title of Book			
Title Page			
Role of Author			

(continued)

	Planning What is my plan?	Reflecting How did I do?	Goal Setting What will I do next time?
Role of Illustrator and Photographer			
Top-to-Bottom Progression			
Left-to-Right Progression			
Return Sweep			
Count Words			
Count Letters in a Word			

A Focus on Alphabet Awareness in Read-Alouds

	Planning What is my plan?	Reflecting How did I do?	Goal Setting What will I do next time?
Identify Any Letter			
Identify Specific Letter/ Letters			
Identify a Letter in Child's Own Name			
Sound–Symbol Correspondence			

A Focus on Phonological Awareness in Read-Alouds

	Planning What is my plan?	Reflecting How did I do?	Goal Setting What will I do next time?
Counting Words			
Segmenting Syllables			
Blending Syllables			

(continued)

	Planning What is my plan?	Reflecting How did I do?	Goal Setting What will I do next time?
Rhyme Identification			
Rhyme Completion			
Rhyme Production			
Alliteration/ Initial Sound Identification			

A Focus on Comprehension Development in Read-Alouds

	Planning What is my plan?	Reflecting How did I do?	Goal Setting What will I do next time?
Prediction Questions			
Open-Ended Questions			
Text-to-Self Connection Questions			
Text-to-Text Connection Questions			
Reflection and Recall Questions			

References

Adams, M. J. (1990). *Learning to read: Thinking and learning about print.* Cambridge, MA: MIT Press.

Aram, D. (2006). Early literacy interventions: The relative roles of storybook reading, alphabetic activities, and their combination. *Reading and Writing: An Interdisciplinary Journal, 19,* 489–515.

Armbruster, B. B., Lehr, F., & Osborn, J. (2003). *A child becomes a reader.* Portsmouth, NH: National Institute for Literacy: RMC Research Corporation.

Ball, E. W., & Blachman, B. A. (1988). Phoneme segmentation training: Effect on reading readiness. *Annals of Dyslexia, 38,* 208–225.

Ball, E. W., & Blachman, B. A. (1991). Does phoneme awareness training kindergarten make a difference in early word recognition and developmental spelling? *Reading Research Quarterly, 26,* 49–66.

Beck, I. J., & McKeown, M. G. (2007). Increasing young low-income children's oral vocabulary repertoires through rich and focused instruction. *Elementary School Journal, 107*(3), 251–271.

Beck, I. J., McKeown, M. G., & Kucan, L. (2002). *Bringing words to life: Robust vocabulary instruction.* New York: Guilford Press.

Biemiller, A. (2001). Teaching vocabulary: Early, direct, and sequential. *American Educator, 25,* 24–28.

Bus, A. G. (2001). Joint caregiver–child storybook reading: A route to literacy development. In S. B. Neuman & D. K. Dickinson (Eds.), *Handbook of early literacy research, Vol. 1* (pp. 179–191). New York: Guilford Press.

Bus, A. G., & van IJzendoorn, M. H. (1995). Mothers reading to their three-year-olds: The role of mother–child attachment security in becoming literate. *Reading Research Quarterly, 40,* 998–1015.

Cardoso-Martins, C., Resende, S. M., & Rodrigues, L. A. (2002). Letter-name knowledge and the ability to learn to read by processing letter–phoneme relations in words: Evidence from

Brazilian Portuguese-speaking children. *Reading and Writing: An Interdisciplinary Journal*, 15, 409–432.

Clay, M. (1991). *Becoming literate*. Portsmouth, NH: Heinemann.

Dole, J. A., Duffy, G. G., Roehler, L. E., & Pearson, P. D. (1991). Moving from the old to the new: Research on reading comprehension instruction. *Review of Educational Research*, 61, 239–264.

Elley, W. B. (1989). Vocabulary acquisition from listening to stories. *Reading Research Quarterly*, 24, 174–187.

Hargrave, A. C., & Senechal, M. (2000). A book reading intervention with preschool children who have limited vocabularies: The benefits of regular reading and dialogic reading. *Early Childhood Research Quarterly*, 15(1), 75–90.

Hart, B., & Risley, R. T. (1995). *Meaningful differences in the everyday experience of young American children*. Baltimore: Brookes.

Hirsch, E. (2006). *The knowledge deficit. Closing the shocking educational gap for American children*. Boston: Houghton Mifflin.

International Reading Association & National Association for the Education of Young Children. (1998). Learning to read and write: Developmentally appropriate practices for young children. *Reading Teacher*, 52, 193–216. (Also available in *Young Children*, 53(4), 75–88)

Johnson, C. J., & Yeates, E. (2006). Evidence-based vocabulary instruction for elementary students via storybook reading. *EBP: A Scholarly Forum for Guiding Evidence-Based Practices in Speech–Language Pathology*, 1(3), 1–23.

Johnson, D. (2009). *The joy of children's literature*. Belmont, CA: Wadsworth, Cengage Learning.

Juel, C. (1988). Learning to read and write: A longitudinal study of 54 children from first through fourth grade. *Journal of Educational Psychology*, 80, 437–447.

Justice, L., Bowles, R., & Skibbe, L. (2006). Measuring preschool attainment of print-concept knowledge: A study of typical and at-risk 3- to 5-year-old children. *Language, Speech, and Hearing Services in Schools*, 37, 224–235.

Justice, L. M., Bowles, R. P., & Skibbe, L. E. (2006). Measuring preschool attainment of print-concept knowledge: A study of typical and at-risk 3- to 5-year-old children using item response theory. *Language, Speech, and Hearing Services in Schools*, 37, 224–235.

Justice, L. M., & Ezell, H. K. (2000). Enhancing children's print and word awareness through home-based parent intervention. *American Journal of Speech Language Pathology*, 9, 257–269.

Justice, L. M., & Ezell, H. K. (2002). Use of storybook reading to increase print awareness in at-risk children. *American Journal of Speech–Language Pathology*, 11, 17–29.

Justice, L. M., & Ezell, H. K. (2004). Print referencing: An emergent literacy enhancement strategy and its clinical applications. *Language, Speech, and Hearing Services in Schools*, 35, 185–193.

Justice, L. M., Kaderavek, J., Bowles, R., & Grimm, K. (2005). Language impairment, parent–child shared reading, and phonological awareness: A feasibility study. *Topics in Early Childhood Special Education*, 25(3), 143–156.

Justice, L. M., & Kaderavek, J. N. (2002). Using shared storybook reading to promote emergent literacy. *Teaching Exceptional Children*, 34, 8–13.

Justice, L. M., Meier, J., & Walpole, S. (2005). Learning new words from storybooks: An efficacy study with at-risk kindergarteners. *Language, Speech, and Hearing Services in Schools*, 36, 17–32.

Justice, L. M., Weber, S. E., Ezell, H. K., & Bakeman, R. (2002). A sequential analysis of children's responsiveness to parental print references during shared book-reading interactions. *American Journal of Speech–Language Pathology*, 11, 30–40.

Lonigan, C. J., Burgess, S. R., Anthony, J. L., & Barker, T. A. (1998). Development of phonological sensitivity in two- to five-year-old children. *Journal of Educational Psychology, 90,* 294–311.

Lovelace, S., & Stewart, S. (2007). Increasing print awareness in preschoolers with language impairment using non-evocative print referencing. *Language, Speech, and Hearing Services in Schools, 38,* 16–30.

McFadden, T. U. (1998). Sounds and stories: Teaching phonemic awareness in print concepts. *American Journal of Speech–Language Pathology, 7,* 5–13.

McGee, L. M., & Purcell-Gates, V. (1997). "So what's going on in research on emergent literacy?" *Reading Research Quarterly, 32,* 310–318.

McGee, L. M., & Schickedanz, J. A. (2007). Repeated interactive read-alouds in preschool and kindergarten. *Reading Teacher, 60*(8), 742–751.

Morris, D., Bloodgood, J., & Perney, J. (2003). Kindergarten predictors of first- and second-grade reading achievement. *Elementary School Journal, 104*(2), 93–109.

Morrow, L. M. (1987). The effect of small group story reading on children's questions and comments. In S. McCormick & J. Zutell (Eds.), *Cognitive and social perspectives for literacy research and instruction: Thirty-seventh yearbook of the National Reading Conference* (pp. 77–86). Chicago, IL: National Reading Conference.

Morrow, L. M. (2001). *Literacy development in the early years: Helping children read and write.* Boston: Allyn & Bacon.

Morrow, L. M. (2004). *Children's literature in preschool: Comprehending and enjoying books.* Newark, DE: International Reading Association.

National Early Literacy Panel. (2007). *Developing early literacy: Report of the National Early Literacy Panel.* Washington, DC: National Institute for Literacy.

National Governors Association Center for Best Practices and Council of Chief State School Officers (2010). Common Core State Standards initiative: Preparing America's students for college and career. Retrieved January 10, 2011, from *www.corestandards.org.*

National Institute of Child Health and Human Development. (2000). Report of the National Reading Panel. Teaching children to read: An evidence-based assessment of the scientific research literature on reading and its implications for reading instruction (NIH Publication No. 00- 4769). Washington, DC: U.S. Government Printing Office.

National Reading Panel. (2000). *Teaching children to read: An evidence-based assessment of the scientific research literature on reading and its implications for reading instruction: Reports of the subgroups.* Washington, DC: U.S. Government Printing Office.

Neuman, S. B. (1999). Books make a difference: A study of access to literacy. *Reading Research Quarterly, 34,* 286–301.

Neuman, S. B., & Celano, D. (2001). Books aloud: A campaign to put books in children's hands. *Reading Teacher, 54,* 550–557.

Neuman, S. B., Copple, C., & Bredekamp, S. (2000). *Learning to read and write: Developmentally appropriate practices for young children.* Washington, DC: National Association for the Education of Young Children.

Paris, A. H., & Paris, S. G. (2003). Assessing narrative comprehension in young children. *Reading Research Quarterly, 38*(1), 36–76.

Pressley, M. (2000). What should comprehension instruction be the instruction of? In M. L. Kamil, P. B. Mosenthal, P. D. Pearson, & R. Barr (Eds.), *Handbook of reading research: Volume III* (pp. 545–561). Mahwah NJ: Erlbaum.

Pressley, M., & Hilden, K. (2002). How can children be taught to comprehend text better? In M.

L. Kamil, J. B. Manning, & H. J. Walberg (Eds.), *Successful reading instruction* (pp. 33–53). Greenwich, CT: Information Age.

Pullen, P., & Justice, L. (2003). Enhancing phonological awareness, print awareness, and oral language skills in preschool children. *Intervention in School and Clinic, 39*(2), 87–98.

Richgels, D. J. (1995). Invented spelling ability and printed word learning in kindergarten. *Reading Research Quarterly, 30,* 96–109.

Robbins, C., & Ehri, L. C. (1994). Reading storybooks to kindergarteners helps them learn new vocabulary words. *Journal of Educational Psychology, 86,* 54–64.

Scott, J. A., & Nagy, W. (2004). Developing word consciousness. In J. F. Baumann & E. J. Kame'enui (Eds.), *Vocabulary instruction: Research to practice* (pp. 201–217). New York: Guilford Press.

Snow, C. E. (2002). *Reading for understanding: Toward a research and development program in reading comprehension.* Pittsburgh: RAND.

Snow, C. E., Burns, M. S., & Griffin, P. (1998). *Preventing reading difficulties in young children.* Washington, DC: National Academy Press.

Stanovich, K. E. (1986). Matthew effects in reading: Some consequences of individual differences in the acquisition of literacy. *Reading Research Quarterly, 21,* 360–406.

Trachtenburg, P., & Ferruggia, A. (1989). Big books from little voices: Reaching high risk beginning readers. *Reading Teacher, 42*(4), 284–289.

Uhry, J. K. (2002). Finger-point reading in kindergarten: The role of phonemic awareness, one-to-one correspondence, and rapid serial naming. *Scientific Studies of Reading, 6,* 319–341.

Ukrainetz, T. A., Cooney, M. H., Dyer, S. H., Kysar, A. J., & Harris, T. J. (2000). An investigation into teaching phonemic awareness through shared reading and writing. *Early Childhood Research Quarterly, 15*(3), 331–355.

Van Kleek, A. (1995). Emphasizing form and meaning separately in prereading and early reading instruction. *Topics in Language Disorders, 16,* 27–49.

Vellutino, F. R., & Scanlon, D. M. (1987). Phonological coding, phonological awareness and reading ability: Evidence from a longitudinal and experimental study. *Merrill–Palmer Quarterly, 33,* 321–363.

Walsh, B., & Blewitt, P. (2006). The effect of questioning style during storybook reading on novel vocabulary acquisition of preschoolers. *Early Childhood Education Journal, 33*(4), 273–278.

Wasik, B. A., Bond, M. A., & Hindman, A. (2006). The effects of a language and literacy intervention on Head Start children and teachers. *Journal of Educational Psychology, 98*(1), 63–74.

Wasik, B. A., & Bond, M. A. (2001). Beyond the pages of a book: Interactive book reading and language development in preschool classrooms. *Journal of Educational Psychology, 93,* 243–250.

Wells, G. (1986). *Language development in the preschool years.* New York: Cambridge University Press.

Whitehurst, G. J., Arnold, D. S., Epstein, J. N., Angell, A. L., Smith, M., & Fischel, J. (1994). A picture book reading intervention in day care and home for children from low-income families. *Developmental Psychology, 30,* 679–689.

Yopp, H. K., & Yopp, R. H. (2000). Supporting phonemic awareness development in the classroom. *Reading Teacher, 54*(2), 130–143.

Children's Books

Aardema, V. (1975). *Why mosquitoes buzz in people's ears: A West African tale*. New York: Dial Press.

Adams, P. (2007). *There was an old lady who swallowed a fly*. Swindon, UK: Child's Play International.

Andreae, G. (1999). *Giraffes can't dance*. New York: Scholastic.

Bloom, B. (1999). *Wolf!* New York: Scholastic.

Bonnett-Rampersaud, L. (2005). *How do you sleep?* New York: Marshall Cavendish Children.

Boynton, S. (1984). *A to Z*. New York: Little Simon.

Bradley, K. B. (2001). *Pop! A book about bubbles*. New York: HarperCollins.

Brett, J. (1997). *The mitten*. New York: Putnam.

Briggs, R. (1978). *The snowman*. New York: Random House.

Bruel, N. (2005). *Bad kitty*. New Milford: Roaring Brook Press.

Cannon, J. (1994). *Stelaluna*. Barcelona: Editorial Juventud.

Carle, E. (1987). *The tiny seed*. Natick, MA: Picture Book Studio.

Carle, E. (2007). *Eric Carle's ABC*. New York: Grosset & Dunlap.

Carney, E. (2009). National Geographic Readers: *Frogs!* Washington, DC: National Geographic.

Cole, H. (1997). *Jack's garden*. New York: Greenwillow Books.

Cole, J., & Calmenson, S. (1990). *Miss Mary Mack and other children's street rhymes*. New York: HarperCollins.

Cooper, S. K. (2007). *Whose hat is this?* Minneapolis: Picture Window Books.

Dahl, R. (1982). *Revolting rhymes*. New York: Puffin Books.

dePaola, T. (1975). *Strega Nona: An old tale*. Englewood Cliffs, NJ: Prentice-Hall.

Dewdney, A. (2007). *Llama llama mad at mama*. New York: Scholastic.

Donaldson, J. (2004). *The snail and the whale*. New York: Dial.

Doran, E. (2005). *A is for artist: An alphabet*. London: Tate Gallery.

Dragonwagon, C. (1992). *Alligator arrived with apples: A potluck alphabet feast*. New York: Aladdin.

Earle, A. (1995). *Zipping, zapping, zooming bats.* New York: HarperCollins.

Eastman, P. D. (1974). *The alphabet book.* New York: Random House Books.

Ehlert, L. (1991). *Red leaf, yellow leaf.* San Diego, CA: Harcourt Brace Jovanovich.

Elting, M., & Folsom, M. (2005). *Q is for duck: An alphabet guessing game.* Boston: Sandpiper.

Ernst, L. C. (2004). *The turn-around, upside-down alphabet book.* New York: Simon & Schuster.

Falk, L. (2009). *This is the way we go to school: A book about children around the world.* New York: Scholastic.

Fleming, D. (1991). *In the tall, tall grass.* New York: Holt.

Fredericks, A. D. (2001). *Under one rock: Bugs, slugs, and other ughs.* Nevada City, CA: Dawn Publications.

Freeman, D. (1968). *Corduroy.* New York: Viking Press.

Freeman, D. (1978). *A pocket for Corduroy.* New York: Viking Press.

Gaiman, N. (2008). *The dangerous alphabet.* New York: HarperCollins.

Gerstein, M. (2001). *The absolutely awful alphabet.* Boston: Sandpiper.

Gibbons, G. (2008). *Ice cream: The full scoop.* New York: Holiday House.

Gramatky, H. (1997). *Little toot.* New York: Grosset & Dunlap.

Gustafson, S. (2007) *Favorite nursery rhymes from mother goose.* Seymour, CT: Greenwich Workshop Press.

Hall, D., & Cooney, B. (1979). *Ox-cart man.* New York: Viking Press.

Hatkoff, C., Hatkoff, J., Hatkoff, I., & Kahumbu, P. (2008). *Looking for Miza: The true story of the mountain gorilla family who rescued one of their own.* New York: Scholastic Press.

Hatkoff, I., Hatkoff, C., & Kahumbu, P. (2006). *Owen & Mzee: The true story of a remarkable friendship.* New York: Scholastic.

Hatkoff, I., Hatkoff, C., & Kahumbu, P. (2007). *Owen & Mzee: The language of friendship.* New York: Scholastic.

Hatkoff, I., Hatkoff, C., & Kahumbu, P. (2008). *Owen & Mzee: A day together.* New York: Scholastic.

Hatkoff, J., Hatkoff, C., & Uhlich G. R. (2007). *Knut: How one little polar bear captivated the world.* London: Scholastic.

Hatkoff, J., Hatkoff, I., & Hatkoff, C. (2009). *Winter's tail: How one little dolphin learned to swim again.* New York: Scholastic.

Henkes, K. (1996). *Lilly's purple plastic purse.* New York: Greenwillow Books.

Henkes, K. (2000). *Wemberly worried.* New York: Greenwillow Books.

Herzog, B. (2004). *H is for home run: A baseball alphabet.* Ann Arbor, MI: Sleeping Bear Press.

Hesse, K. (1999). *Come on, rain!* New York: Scholastic.

Hogrogian, N. (1971). *One fine day.* New York: Macmillan.

Iorio, N. (2005a). *Time for kids: Bats!* New York: HarperCollins.

Iorio, N. (2005b). *Time for kids: Spiders!.* New York: HarperCollins.

Jay, A. (2003). *ABC: A child's first alphabet book.* New York: Dutton Juvenile.

Jenkins, S. (2003). *What do you do with a tail like this?* Boston: Houghton Mifflin.

Johnson, S. T. (1999). *Alphabet city.* New York: Puffin.

Juster, N. (2005). *The hello, goodbye window.* New York: Michael di Capua Books/Hyperion Books for Children.

Kalman, B. (2007). *Is it a living thing?* New York: Crabtree.

Keats, E. J. (1962). *The snowy day.* New York: Viking Press.

Keats, E. J. (1998). *Peter's chair.* New York: Viking.

Kontis, A. (2006). *Alphaoops! The day Z went first.* Somerville, MA: Candlewick.

Kraft, E. (2008). *Chocolatina*. New York: Cartwheel Books.

Kramer, S. (1995). *Caves*. Minneapolis: Carolrhoda Books.

Lehn, B. (1999). *What is a scientist?* Brookfield, CT: Millbrook Press.

Levenson, G. (2002). *Pumpkin circle: The story of a garden*. Berkeley, CA: Tricycle Press.

Levine, E. (1993). *If your name was changed at Ellis Island*. New York: Scholastic.

Lobel, A. (1981). *On market street*. New York: Greenwillow Books.

Martin, B., Jr., & Archambault, J. (2009). *Chicka chicka boom boom: Anniversary edition*. La Jolla, CA: Beach Lane Books.

McBratney, S. (1995). *Guess how much I love you*. Cambridge, MA: Candlewick Press.

McGovern, A. (1992). *If you lived in colonial times*. New York: Scholastic.

McLeod, B. (2008). *Superhero ABC*. New York: HarperCollins.

McPhail, D. (1996). *Pigs aplenty, pigs galore!* New York: Puffin.

Miller, J. (2000). *The farm alphabet book*. New York: Scholastic.

Moore, I. (1993). *Six-dinner Sid*. New York: Simon & Schuster Books for Young Readers.

Munsch, R. N. (1992). *The paper bag princess*. Buffalo, NY: Discis Knowledge Research.

Munsch, R. N. (1996). *Stephanie's ponytail*. Toronto: Annick Press.

Munson, D. (2000). *Enemy pie*. San Francisco: Chronicle Books.

Nevius, C. (2008). *Baseball hour*. New York: Cavendish.

Numeroff, L. J. (1998). *If you give a pig a pancake*. New York: Geringer Books.

Numeroff, L. J. (2000). *If you take a mouse to the movies*. New York: Geringer Books.

Numeroff, L. J. (2002). *If you take a mouse to school*. New York: Geringer Books/HarperCollins.

Pallotta, J. (1991). *The underwater alphabet book*. Watertown, MA: Charlesbridge.

Pelletier, D. (1996). *The graphic alphabet*. New York: Scholastic.

Peterson, M., & Rofe, J. (2010). *Piggies in the pumpkin patch*. Watertown, MA: Charlesbridge.

Pfeffer, W. (2007). *A log's life*. New York: Simon & Schuster Books for Young Readers.

Piper, W., & Long, L. (2005). *The little engine that could*. New York: Philomel Books.

Polacco, P. (1998). *Thank you, Mr. Falker*. New York: Philomel Books.

Prelutsky, J. (2008). *Be glad your nose is on your face and other poems*. New York: Greenwillow Books.

Rathmann, P. (1995). *Officer Buckle and Gloria*. New York: Putnam.

Rose, D. L. (2000). *Into the A, B, sea: An ocean alphabet book*. New York: Scholastic.

Rylant, C. (1985). *The relatives came*. New York: Bradbury Press.

Rylant, C. (1982). *When I was young in the mountains*. New York: Puffin.

Rylant, C. (2000). *The old woman who named things*. San Diego, CA: Harcourt Brace.

Sandved, K. B. (1999). *The butterfly alphabet*. New York: Scholastic.

Scanlon, L. G. (2009). *All the world*. New York: Beach Lane Books.

Schachner, J. B. (1999). *The grannyman*. New York: Dutton Children's Books.

Seeger, L. V. (2006). *Walter was worried*. New York: Roaring Brook Press.

Seuss, Dr. (1960). *One fish two fish red fish blue fish*. New York: Random House.

Seuss, Dr. (1996). *Dr. Seuss's ABC: An amazing alphabet book!* New York: Random House Books.

Shannon, D. (1998). *A bad case of stripes*. New York: Blue Sky Press.

Shannon, D. (1999). *David goes to school*. New York: Blue Sky Press.

Shannon, G. (1999). *Tomorrow's alphabet*. New York: Greenwillow Books.

Shaw, N. (2006). *Sheep in a jeep*. Boston: Sandpiper.

Silverstein, S. (2004). *Where the sidewalk ends*. New York: HarperCollins.

Simon, S. (2007). *Spiders*. New York: HarperCollins.

Simon, S. (2008). *Animals nobody loves*. Paw Prints.

Slobodkina, E. (1947). *Caps for sale: A tale of a peddler, some monkeys and their monkey business*. New York: Scott.

Small, D. (1989). *Imogene's antlers*. New York: Crown.

Smith, K. (2004). *Why don't elephants live in the city?* Columbus, OH: Waterbird Books.

Smith, R. M. (2008). *An A to Z walk in the park*. Alexandria, VA: Clarence-Henry Books.

Sobel, J. (2009). *Shiver me letters: A pirate ABC*. Boston: Sandpiper.

Steig, W. (1982). *Doctor De Soto*. New York: Farrar, Straus, Giroux.

Steig, W. (1986). *Brave Irene*. New York: Farrar, Straus, Giroux.

Steig, W. (2005). *Sylvester and the magic pebble*. New York: Simon & Schuster Books for Young Readers.

Van Allsburg, C. (1987). *The Z was zapped: A play in twenty-six acts*. Boston: Houghton Mifflin.

Viorst, J. (2009). *Alexander and the terrible horrible, no good, very bad day*. New York: Atheneum Books for Young Readers.

Whitcomb, M. (1998). *Odd velvet*. San Francisco: Chronicle Books.

Willems, M. (2003). *Don't let the pigeon drive the bus*. New York: Hyperion Books for Children.

Willems, M. (2004). *Knuffle bunny: A cautionary tale*. New York: Hyperion Books for Children.

Willems, M. (2005). *The pigeon has feelings, too!: A smidgeon of a pigeon*. New York: Hyperion Books for Children.

Willems, M. (2010). *We are in a book!* New York: Hyperion Books.

Williams, V. B. (1984). *A chair for my mother*. New York: Greenwillow Books.

Wood, A. (2001). *Alphabet adventure*. New York: Blue Sky Press.

Wood, A. (2002). *Sweet dream pie*. New York: Blue Sky Press.

Wood, A. (2003). *Alphabet mystery*. New York: Blue Sky Press.

Wood, A. (2006). *Alphabet rescue*. New York: Blue Sky Press.

Wood, A. (2007). *Silly sally*. New York: Houghton Mifflin Harcourt.

Yashima, T. (1955). *Crow boy*. New York: Viking Press.

Yolen, J. (1987). *Owl moon*. New York: Philomel Books.

Yolen, J. (2005). *How do dinosaurs eat their food?* New York: Scholastic.

Young, J. (2006). *Look how it changes!* New York: Children's Press.

Zollman, P. (2005a). *A bear cub grows up*. New York: Children's Press.

Zollman, P. (2005b). *A spiderling grows up*. New York: Children's Press.

Zollman, P. (2005c). *A tadpole grows up*. New York: Children's Press.

Zollman, P. (2005d). *A turtle hatching grows up*. New York: Children's Press.

Index

Page numbers in italics indicate figures.